Biblical Thinking for Building Healthy Churches

IX 9Marks Journal

I0158607

info@9marks.org | www.9marks.org

Tools like this are provided by the generous investment of donors.
Each gift to 9Marks helps equip church leaders with a biblical vision and practical
resources for displaying God's glory to the nations through healthy churches.

Donate at: www.9marks.org/donate.

Or make checks payable to "9Marks" and mail to:
9 Marks
525 A St. NE
Washington, DC 20002

Editorial Director: Jonathan Leeman
Managing Editor: Taylor Hartley
Editors: Alex Duke and David Daniels
Proof Reader: Judith Henderson
Executive Director: Ryan Townsend
President: Mark Dever
Cover Design: OpenBox9
Paperback: 978-1-958168-73-8
eBook: 978-1-958168-69-1

Editor's Note

Jonathan Leeman

I f you've spent any time in 9Marks' circles, you might have heard a slight note of skepticism around the topic of programs or church ministries. The note is played because we're dedicated to the whole church gathering and the ordinary means of grace, and we don't want anything to distract from that.

That said, children's ministries, youth ministries, other age-specific ministries, small groups, and gender-specific ministries can do good discipling work. So how can churches employ them well? For a church that wants to keep the main gathering primary in its discipleship and life together, what are the hallmarks of healthy ministries?

We asked a host of pastors for their wisdom. We pray their experience might serve you.

Jonathan (@JonathanLeeman) edits the 9Marks series of books as well as the 9Marks Journal. He is also the author of several books on the church. Since his call to ministry, Jonathan has earned a master of divinity from Southern Seminary and a Ph.D. in Ecclesiology from the University of Wales. He lives with his wife and four daughters in Cheverly, Maryland, where he is an elder at Cheverly Baptist Church.

A Foolproof Discipling Program: Corporate Worship

John Sarver

Regardless of how your church states its mission—"living and proclaiming God's truth in the world" or "spreading a passion for God's supremacy among the nations"—every biblical church exists to make disciples, that is, gospel-believing, Spirit indwelt, Word-obeying, Kingdom-advancing followers of Jesus Christ. This goal can be stated in different ways and with different emphases. It can be cute or curt. The bottom line is churches make disciples.

Okay … but *how* does a church do this? How does *your church* do this?

A thought experiment might help us here. Let's say someone is converted through a relationship with a member of your church. What do you do next? Do you put them through a class for new Christians? Rush to place them in a community group? Maybe you've read *The Trellis and the Vine* (ah, that's where I remember this illustration) and you enlist that member to begin discipling them.

All that's wonderful. Now let me ask a follow-up question: what does your church's weekly corporate worship gathering have to do with that baby believer's discipleship? Further still, what's the relationship between that newly formed discipling relationship and the Sunday service? More to the point, does your church make disciples when it gathers or only when its members scatter?

If you do a quick Google search, or thumb through your favorite publisher's most recent catalog, or pick up the latest popular book on discipleship, you'll find a consistent theme: *real discipling work* happens either through well-constructed programs or organic personal ministry.

I don't intend to disparage programs or discipling. A culture of discipling—where members do deliberate spiritual good to one another out of a sense of loving obligation—is *necessary* for a church to be healthy. Programs can help toward that end.

But I am concerned that many pastors unwittingly overlook the core discipleship program the New Testament prescribes: the corporate worship gathering. It's more fundamental to Christian growth than any program. Yes, it's even more fundamental than any personal ministry of the Word that ought to resound throughout the week. The Sunday gathering is the *primary discipler* of a local congregation. Why? Because of what it **proclaims** and the **pattern** it sets.

PROCLAMATION: THE GATHERING DISCIPLES

When saints gather on Sundays, they do so to worship, yes, and to grow. And God grows his people through the Word—his world-creating, life-maintaining, saint-sanctifying Word (John 1:3-4; Heb. 1:1; John 17:17; 2 Tim. 3:16). It's no surprise, then, that Scripture regulates the service around itself. In the gathering, we should read and preach Holy Scripture (1 Tim. 4:13; 2 Tim. 4:1–3), we should sing its truths (Col. 3:16), we should pray its hopes (Eph. 6:18), and we should visualize its message through the sacraments (1 Cor. 11:26; 10:21).

A Sunday morning gathering isn't a production. It's not marked by pageantry or sophistry. No. saints gather every Lord's Day trusting their pastors have planned a service that delivers up their most important meal of the week.

In other words, the corporate worship gathering disciples the saints because it proclaims God's Word which in turn teaches for growth and trains for ministry. These saints are then called to teach what they've heard in the presence of the assembly (2 Tim. 3:16-17).

PATTERN: THE GATHERING TRAINS

Think about what you want your church's discipling relationships and programs to look like. You want to equip Christians to read and teach Scripture, to repent of sin, to increase in grace-driven holiness, and to learn how to better bear each other's burdens and sorrows. The Sunday service not only hones these disciplines, it also models how to do them.

Through thoughtful and protracted prayers of praise, confession, thanksgiving, and supplication, saints are taught how to pray for and with one another. They're shown how to recount God's deeds. They're shown how to confess their sin in anticipation of forgiveness. They're tutored in praying for missionaries, their city, other churches, and their fellow members.

Because Scripture regulates the service, saints are taught to listen when God speaks. And since good preachers not only explain the text but interpret and illustrate the Scripture, saints are taught how to read, study, and teach God's Word themselves. Through faithful application, they're taught how to confront and comfort one another with the Bible. Faithful preaching not only sustains the saints but trains them up as teachers.

Through the sacraments, the body is reminded that the Christian life is marked by repentance of sin and faith in Christ (Rom. 6:1–11). The many members are bound as one body through the bread (1 Cor. 10:17), and they are clearly marked off from the world (Matt. 28:19; see also 1 Cor. 5:9–13).

What should the saints do in community groups, discipling relationships, Sunday schools, and during family worship? Some combination of studying Scripture, praising God, confessing sin, and pursuing one another for the edification of the individual and the whole. Put simply, they should do what they see on Sundays. They should speak what they hear. Individual members should imitate the corporate model. After all, healthy gatherings will over time produce healthy disciples, and weak services over time will produce weak disciples—or teach them to look for necessary edification elsewhere.

REVERBERATION: FROM THE GATHERING TO THE REST

The biblical pattern for church ministry moves from the pulpit to the people, from the gathering to the scattering.[1] Never the other way around. All other ministries should be subservient to and ordered around the church's main gathering. It's intended to be the roaring river that gives life and direction to all the other discipling tributaries of the church. The order is never reversed.

Ephesians 4 says that Christ has ascended to fill all things (Eph. 4:9–10). From his glorious session, he gives to his church. Notably, Paul marks out teaching gifts: apostles, prophets, pastors, and teachers (v. 11). They're given to equip the saints for the work of the ministry which is for the building up the body of Christ (v. 12). The pastors teach and train the saints. And then *the members do what their pastors do*: they speak the truth in love (v. 15). Both preaching and speaking are necessary for the entire body to grow into maturity.

But notice one is primary—both temporally and functionally. Discipling flows from the pastors to the people. From Sunday to every other day of the week. Every discipling conversation, every Bible study, every counseling appointment, and every evening of family worship echoes the Word as its taught and modeled on Sundays. This is the basic shape of biblical ministry: the church gathers and then scatters; the saints rest and then work; the pastors preach and then the people parrot. One discipling event leads to and orders the rest.

PRIORITIZE THE GATHERING

So prioritize the gathering. Read Scripture in your gathering knowing that God uses it to save souls and sustain faith. Model for your members what they ought to do at home and in their classes. Do multiple readings. Read whole chapters. Recite Scripture corporately.

Pray in your gathering. Pray knowing it increases your members' trust in God and their communion with him. Pray like you want the saints to

---

1 On this point see Jonathan Leeman, *Word-Centered Church: How Scripture Brings Life and Growth to God's People* (Chicago: Moody Publishers, 2017).

pray with and for one another: praising God, confessing sin, pleading for the lost, lifting-up neighboring churches, and interceding for their brothers and sisters by name.

And preach. Preach knowing God speaks through you to raise the dead, stir the idle, encourage the faithful, feed the hungry, and mend the wounded. Preach in such a way that your members leave better equipped to teach one another. Exposit the text. Answer difficult questions. Interpret Scripture with Scripture. And apply it to your church.

How does a church make disciples? Through its corporate gathering. While the gathering isn't sufficient to bring saints to full maturity in Christ, it's the engine that drives all those other good efforts.

John Sarver is a pastor of Midtown Baptist Church in Memphis, Tennessee.

I Hear There Are Divisions Among You: Moving Away from Music-Specific Services

Allen Duty

"Traditional Service, 9:00 a.m; Contemporary Service, 11:00 a.m."

If you do a quick search online for churches in your area, chances are that at least some of them have multiple services. And among churches that have multiple services, many of them have "music-specific services."

A "music-specific service" is a worship service where the primary difference between it and the other worship service(s) at the same church is the style of music and the type of songs. I believe churches should move away from these kinds of services. My reason is simple: *music-specific services actively promote division in the body of Christ.*

Very often, that division shows up demographically, with older saints tending toward the traditional-music services and younger saints toward the contemporary. And each group misses the goodness the other group has to offer.

DIVIDED BY TUNE

In 1 Corinthians 1:10, Paul writes, "I appeal to you, brothers, by the name of our Lord Jesus Christ, that all of you agree, and that there be no divisions among you, but that you be united in the same mind and the same judgment."

Paul appeals to the Corinthians to eliminate divisions in their church and pursue unity instead. But when we offer music-specific services, we encourage Christians who are members of the same church to divide according to musical preference. If God has a problem with us dividing over our favorite preachers (the context of 1 Corinthians 1), how must he feel about us dividing over hymns and praise choruses, pianos and guitars, older and newer songs? I have to think Paul's correction applies here as well: "What shall I say to you? Shall I commend you in this? No, I will not" (1 Cor. 11:22).

In John 4:24, Jesus tells the woman at the well, "God is spirit, and those who worship him must worship in spirit and truth." When Jesus uses the word "worship," he has more in mind than just singing. But since we're commanded to sing as part of our worship (Col. 3:16, Eph. 5:19), we can conclude that the words we sing (truth) and the posture of our hearts while we sing (spirit) are the most important aspects of our singing.

If we can agree on that, then we should also be able to agree that the kinds of songs we sing, the way they are arranged, and the way they are sung are less important. We should prioritize singing what is true about God and what he has done on our behalf in Christ, and we should de-emphasize the importance of the kinds of songs we sing and the way they are accompanied. As Matt Merker writes in *Corporate Worship*:

> As a people reconciled to God and one another, we should showcase our peace when we gather to sing. Our love matters more than our preferences. Pastors, therefore, should teach members to engage with the singing whether or not a certain song is in their favorite style. These days, we can all listen to our favorite music in headphones whenever we want. But when we gather on the Lord's Day, we can display that the bonds of Christ are stronger than shared cultural background or musical opinions. (144-145)

So, if you pastor a church that has music-specific services and you've been convinced that it's not best for your congregation, what should you do?

HOW TO REUNITE YOUR CHURCHES

First, you should do nothing—at least not right away. Chances are your church has had music-specific services for years, possibly decades. They didn't get there overnight, and you shouldn't try to change things overni-ght. That would be both unwise and unloving.

Second, you should pray for your church's unity, and pray for this publicly. They're called "worship *wars*" for a reason—people have strong opinions about music. But it doesn't have to be war and, according to Scripture, it shouldn't. It would be naïve to think you can make changes to the music at your church without any friction or disagreement, but that doesn't mean it has to be divisive. Pray that God would give the leaders and members of your church a unified vision and the humility required to lay down preferences for one another (Phil. 2:3).

Third, you should listen to members of your congregation, especially those who have been in leadership for some time. Fools rush in, but wise leaders seek to understand why things are the way they are. Ask good questions about when the church began music-specific services, why they began, and who led the change. It's likely that the changes were made with good motives—such as wanting to honor the preferences of other saints, not wanting to distract from more important matters, or wanting to reach unchurched people. Those are all commendable motives, even if the decisions based on those motives promote disunity.

Fourth, you should teach your congregation about the purpose of corporate worship from Scripture. It's ironic that churches of all types spend so much time, energy, and money on worship in song, but many Christians have never heard any teaching on the subject. When I preached on the role of singing in corporate worship last year, I was surprised by the number of church members who told me they had been in church their whole lives and never heard a single sermon about singing. Don't assume that your church members know what the Bible teaches about singing in worship. If my experience is any indication, many do not.

Only after you've waited, prayed, listened, and taught should you seek to lead change at your church. Again, going "cold turkey" and transitioning overnight is probably unwise. Be patient with those who are accustomed to and enjoy one particular worship style. Make gradual changes over time, and continue to pray, listen to, and teach the members of your church. Such work is never finished.

CONCLUSION

Having music-specific services doesn't promote unity. In fact, it builds preferential division into the structure of the church. If you agree, then I hope you'll do nothing about it. And then I hope you'll pray, listen, teach, and lead your congregation to change.

Allen Duty is the preaching pastor at New Life Baptist Church in College Station, Texas. You can find him on Twitter at @AllenDuty.

The Empty Promises of a Busy Ministry Schedule

Justin Perdue

When visitors show up at a church gathering, I often hear a version of this question: "What do you have for _____?" Children? Youth? Singles? Men? Women? Seniors? They assume that a good church has a lot of programs for specific subsets of people. Programs are how people get plugged in and grow. Surely, underneath the musculature of a healthy church, we find the skeletal system of a full ministry calendar, right?

In fact, a busy ministry calendar can distract and exhaust the saints more than it establishes them in the faith and furthers the church's mission.

The aim of this article is not to discourage any and all programs or extra activities in a church. Instead, the goal is to emphasize the primary things revealed to us in Scripture that have also withstood the test of time.

I want to consider two theological problems that mislead us into thinking that a busy ministry calendar produces maturity in Christ, and then offer three encouragements for how to structure your church's ministries.

THEOLOGICAL PROBLEM #1: DERIVING OUR IDENTITY FROM WHAT WE DO

Being a pastor, I often ask people about how they are doing. It is remarkable how many immediately respond with a list of things they are doing. Instead of learning how it's going trusting Christ as a pilgrim in this fallen world, I get an update on how frequently quiet times are happening, what books are being read, and their recent attendance at a community group. This is a dead giveaway that we've been conditioned to regard our Christian identity by what we're doing.

Biblically speaking, the Christian life is a given life. We receive the righteousness and satisfaction of Christ by faith (Romans 3:21–26, 5:12–21; Philippians 3:1–11). We are united to him. We then live from our union with Christ and our justified status, but we are not chasing after anything (Romans 5:1–11, 6:1–23, 8:1–4, 15–17). Everything we do, we do in view of God's mercy, not in the hope of attaining it.[2]

THEOLOGICAL PROBLEM #2: WE DON'T THINK THE ORDINARY MEANS OF GRACE WILL DO THE JOB

The church has historically understood that the Lord imparts, sustains, and strengthens his people through the ministry of the Word and the administration of the sacraments—as well as prayer and song.[3] In our day, we tend not to trust that an ordinary life in the fellowship of the saints, participating in the ordinary means of grace, will lead to maturity in Christ.

Or maybe it's not that we don't trust the ordinary means of grace. Maybe we're bored with them. We're looking for the next big thing. We live on a constant quest for spiritual experiences or the key that will unlock true discipleship. And we often think we can find it in some niche ministry in the church.

Having said all this, let me offer three encouragements for your church's ministries.

1. Unashamedly emphasize and prioritize the corporate gathering on the Lord's Day.

When we gather as Christ's people on the Lord's Day, we do so to receive from Christ—his ministry and gifts. We come sinful; he forgives us. We come dirty; he cleans us. We come hungry; he feeds us. We come empty; he fills us.

Corporate worship is an opportunity to hear from and be changed by God. He has spoken. He has revealed himself. He has acted. He has

---

2 This is how the apostles write in the New Testament epistles. They ground the saints in their union with Christ, affirm their adopted and justified status, and then go on to write of how the redeemed live. Notably, consider Romans, Ephesians, Colossians, and 1 John (where John affirms the saints throughout).

3 Matthew 26:26–28; Luke 22:19–20; John 6:47–51; Romans 6:3–5; 10:14–17, 16:25–27; 1 Corinthians 10:16, 11:23–26; Ephesians 4:1–16; Colossians 2:11–12, 3:16; 2 Timothy 3:16–4:2; 1 Peter 3:20–22.

remembered us. He has saved us. And so we respond. This is the most genuinely redemptive thing we do each week. God has promised to be with us, to minister to us, and to give us whatever our faith and love might lack.[4]

Given this, the ministry schedule in our churches should be subservient to the Lord's Day gathering. It also should flow from it, which leads me to my second encouragement...

2. The Lord's Day gathering should equip the saints for the work of ministry. Have a church calendar that allows the saints to minister both to one another and their neighbors.[5]

In our day, it's normal to do life at a breakneck pace. People's lives are full. Admittedly, we sometimes do this to ourselves, but not always. I'm thankful to be a part of a church where many of us are trying to live simple lives oriented around the local church. But even with that, it's still easy to become overwhelmed by everything on our respective family calendars. I trust our church is not unique.

This raises an important question: are we serving our people well by filling up their calendars with a bunch of church activities? If modern life is a rat race, then the contemporary Christian life can often feel like a hamster wheel. We run like crazy. We're doing a lot of stuff. But then we look up, exhausted, but aren't sure if we've gotten anywhere.

It's good to make room during the week for the saints to get together for coffee, a meal, a walk, or a play date at the park. We should make room during the week for the saints to practice hospitality. These kinds of interactions encourage the saints to confess sins to one another; to bear one another's burdens; to invite correction; to encourage, exhort, and admonish one another; and to seek the salvation of their family, friends, and neighbors.

Do our church ministry schedules foster or preclude this kind of activity?

---

4 See the Scripture references on the ordinary means of grace (above), as well as Matthew 11:28-30, 2 Corinthians 3:5-6, 16-18, etc.

5 See, again, Ephesians 4:7-16; Romans 12:3-8; 1 Corinthians 12:1-31. Regarding the significance of ministering to one another and our neighbor, also see Romans 13:8-10, Galatians 6:1-2, etc.

3. Outside the Lord's Day gathering, everything else is a wisdom call. Really.

Our churches are not in sin for having or not having a youth group, a seniors' ministry, community groups, or a women's Bible study. There is a lot of latitude and liberty regarding programmatic ministries in the church.

To the elders at our church, it seems wise to provide additional times outside of Sunday morning for teaching and prayer, so we have two Wednesday nights a month where we learn doctrine, a prayer meeting every Sunday night, and catechism classes every Sunday morning. Outside of those, our other church activities serve as opportunities for the saints to deepen relationships with one another and are structured accordingly.

Here's the question we should ask ourselves about any ministry in the church: Does this ministry clearly serve the church's mission? If it doesn't, feel free to get rid of it. Programs and ministries come and go. Think that way. Talk that way. Structure your budget that way.

A FINAL WORD OF ENCOURAGEMENT

The primary ministry of any church member is to show up to the Lord's Day gathering. Everything else flows from that. There are countless times over the seven years of our church's life that I have said to well-intentioned saints, "Trust Christ. Calm down. And show up to church." Sometimes I add, "And talk to me in a year."

That simple exhortation has been remarkably fruitful in our congregation. Why? Because the Lord builds his church through the means he has given. We can trust him.

Justin Perdue is the lead pastor of Covenant Baptist Church in Arden, North Carolina.

Catering to Ministry Consumers

Josh Hayward

"**W**hat you win people with is what you win them to."
This motto warns against seeker-sensitive church growth methods. "Try to get people *in* through what appeals to their wants (good music, lots of programs, relevant sermons), and then—once they're *in*—give them what they *need* (deep discipleship, sound doctrine)."

The problem with this approach: if people *come* for catchy music or feel-good sermons, then that's what they'll expect to continue. And if you don't supply it, they'll likely be unhappy.

I imagine most pastors reading this article do not have an explicit philosophy of ministry that is seeker-sensitive. You're not saying, "We are intentionally trying to appeal to the wants and desires of non-Christians or baby Christians so that they come to church to hear the gospel."

However, it's easy to cater to consumers in our ministries. Rather, we should shepherd consumers to develop spiritual tastebuds for the ordinary means of grace: the faithful preaching of the Word, the observing of the ordinances, meaningful membership, deep-discipleship, and the like.

KINDS OF CONSUMERS

Before you can shepherd a consumer, you need to know the kind of consumer you're shepherding. There are various kinds. Let me name four.

1. The Event Consumer

The sum and substance of church life for this consumer is the Sunday worship gathering; and not just the gathering itself, but a good production that provides a moving experience. The "event consumer" tends to be passive in his church involvement outside of the Sunday service. He simply wants to show up on Sundays and be filled up for the week.

2. The Theology/Bible Consumer

Yes, such a person exists! This kind of consumer doesn't care too much about relationships, discipleship, evangelism, or any other aspects of church life. They simply want more Bible!

Is that bad? Yes and no. Of course, we want people to want more Bible. But that's all the "Bible consumer" wants. He's not interested in helping others follow Christ. He just wants to fill his head with more Bible knowledge.

The "theology/Bible consumer" also tends to be overly critical about the church because he focuses all his attention on theological precision and consumption.

3. The Relationship Consumer

This is the kind of person who desires to experience community in the church. Again, that's a good thing!

However, when that becomes the only thing we want from a church, it becomes a bad thing. The relational consumer tends to care too little about doctrine. They tend to be a relational taker, rather than a relational giver; meaning, there is little pouring into others through encouragement and service, yet there remains an expectation of being poured into by others.

4. The Ministry Consumer

The ministry consumer wants more trellises, more programs, more structures, more stuff to do. They love to serve the Lord. Amen! But the ministry consumer tends to be difficult to please. They often resist change in their most beloved ministries, yet find much area for improvement in others' ministries.

At the bottom of all such ministry consumption can be self-focus. They can be sinfully discontent because they're not having *their* desires met. They can be overly opinionated because they believe *their* opinion matters most. Those who are overly critical are so because they believe *they* have all the right answers.

There are other kinds of consumers in the church, but, in my experience, these tend to be the most common. And yet, of the four, the ministry consumer is perhaps the most common at least in the West. Because of that, we'll focus our attention there.

THOU SHALT NOT CATER

It is very easy to fall into the trap of catering to ministry consumers. But pastors who do this risk burnout. They're tossed to and fro by the whims of others' wants, and pastors will never be able to satisfy them.

Moreover, as a pastor, if you try to cater to the wants of ministry consumers, you might fall into the trap of relying on methods and programs for spiritual transformation that the Bible simply does not prescribe.

CARING FOR CONSUMERS

If pastors shouldn't cater to ministry consumers, what should they do? The answer is simple: they should do what God has called them to do: *pastor* them. Here are a few tips on pastoring the ministry consumer:

1. Connect them with someone to disciple them.

Perhaps you know of someone in your church who used to be a ministry consumer but is now convinced of pursuing the ordinary means of grace in the life of the church as the pathway to spiritual growth. Connect that person with the ministry consumer. Or simply ask if they would be open to meeting with a godly person on a regular basis to talk through these things and encourage them in Christ.

2. Celebrate the ordinary means of grace.

One vital way to help the ministry consumer move away from a consumeristic mindset is to celebrate the ordinary means of grace in the life of the church. Present before them a vision of just how glorious simple, ordinary church life is. Sunday worship brings together people from various kinds of ethnicities and cultures and ages and backgrounds and baggage into one unified gathering. Such different people then *hear* the power of the Word heralded, *see* a transformed life in baptism, *partake* of the family meal in the Lord's Supper, *sing* together the glories of our God, and *pray* with one voice about this broken world.

Present also a vision of how beautiful a culture of discipleship is in the church. Talk to the church about the impact it has on a single mom when an empty nester, on her own initiative, reaches out to help bring the kids to church, babysit, or just to be someone to talk to and a shoulder to cry on. There's great power in organic discipleship like this!

3. Be a steady presence.

Try not to get tossed to and fro by the varying desires of ministry consumers. They need a pastor who is steady in his conviction—not mean, uncaring, or deaf to their concerns, but nevertheless, steady and firm.

4. Encourage them to find a church that better fits their preferences.

This tip, of course, is the last resort. If someone simply remains unconvinced of a simple ministry schedule and unsatisfied with what is offered, it might be best to encourage them to find a church that better suits their preferences. They might better flourish in that context.

CONCLUSION

What you feed people with is what they'll continue to hunger for. Pastors, strive to cultivate an appetite in the hearts of your people for the ordinary means of grace. Guard your heart against trying to please ministry consumers. Instead, rest in what God has prescribed in his Word, and pastor accordingly.

Josh Hayward serves as senior pastor of Kinney Avenue Christians Fellowship in Austin, Texas. He received his undergraduate degree in Biblical Studies from Moody Bible Institute and his M.Div. in Biblical Counseling from The Southern Baptist Theological Seminary. He is married to Christina, his high school sweetheart, and they have four sons and one daughter.

Preacher, What's on Your Kids Menu?

John Joseph

My family loves to eat out. Burger joints, Thai food, sushi, pizza, whatever. Fine dining or fast food. If you can name it, we've likely eaten it. And in our extensive amount of gastronomic experiences, one thing has been true of every restaurant: they all had a kids menu.

I mean, even fast-food restaurants, whose entire menu is essentially a gigantic kids menu, have a special section *just* for kids. McDonald's Happy Meals anyone? Restaurants understand that if they can't feed kids, then they won't appeal to families and those families will find another restaurant.

I bring this up because when most parents come to a new church, they ask the pastor the same question they ask the restaurant hostess. What's on your kids menu? They want to know if you have spiritual food for their children. Thankfully, most churches do have a kids menu. On it are things like children's ministry classes, Vacation Bible School, youth group, and Awana. But one menu item is often absent: the sermon.

Yes, I realize that basically, all churches have a sermon. My concern is that many (most?) sermons don't have anything for the kids. In that sense, the sermon isn't just a menu item. It's a veritable restaurant unto itself. So let me ask the same question to preachers about their sermons: Preacher, what's on your kids menu?

Do you address kids in your sermons on a regular basis? Do you take time to explain certain things in such a way that kids can understand? When you help adults in your congregation think about how to apply the text to their lives, do you also help kids?

As you labor in the study to put together a feast for your congregation on Sundays, remember to include menu items that kids can eat as well. In order to help you do that, I want to share with you three menu items I have regularly included in my preaching that have, by God's grace, caused the kids to engage more with the sermons and grow in love for God's Word. The great thing about these is that you already have them in your preaching pantry. You just need to prepare them a bit differently for the kids.

1. QUESTIONS

The first menu item I want to encourage you to include in your preaching is questions. Make a habit of asking the kids questions about the text. Call them out as a group. Say something like, "Kids, I have a question for you. Can any of you tell me...?"

You'll want to think about the ages of the kids in your congregation and the types of questions they would be capable of answering. Given that kids' cognitive abilities develop quickly, you might even think about asking questions to specific groups of kids. "I have a question for the 5–7-year-olds... for the 7–10-years-olds... for the 10–13 year-olds... for the teenager..." Be as specific as you like, just be sure to vary it up.

I'm currently preaching through Genesis and have asked all sorts of questions to the kids. When talking about God being a shield, I asked the younger kids what shields are used for. When talking about the covenant God made with Noah, I asked the teens to name the major covenants of the Old Testament. While explaining why Lot and Abram separated, I asked the kids what would happen if I put 10 of them in a room with only enough toys for two of them. In response, they correctly yelled, "We would fight!"

The payoff of this simple practice is huge because kids love answering questions. Eyes will light up, and hands will shoot up. Consistently dripping in a couple of questions every week will do wonders for their engagement.

2. ILLUSTRATIONS

The second menu item I want to encourage you to include for kids is age-appropriate illustrations. Illustrations are important for everyone in the congregation, but especially for the kids. They not only capture their attention but can bring to life glorious biblical truths they might otherwise miss.

Here's the thing though: when you're preparing illustrations for kids, you need to use kid-friendly ingredients. This probably won't come as a surprise to you, but illustrations drawn from your marriage, your work, or current events can be just as difficult for kids to process as the biblical truths you're trying to illustrate. When you're working on an illustration for kids, think about the types of things that capture their imagination.

When talking about our powerlessness to defeat sin, paint a picture for the little boys that shows how impossible it would be to defeat a massive army if they only had nerf guns and plastic swords. When talking to teen girls, tell them to imagine how amazing it would be if they were friends with Taylor Swift and could call her anytime they wanted. Then tell them how much more amazing it is that they're friends with *God* and can talk to *him* whenever they want. If you want children to know how much grace God pours out on us, tell them about the giant water bucket at Great Wolf Lodge that, when poured out, regularly knocks kids off their feet. (Check it out on YouTube if you don't know what I'm talking about!)

From Daniel Tiger to Narnia, from Dude Perfect to amusement parks, from feeling scared in the dark to getting caught doing something wrong, the list of ways to illustrate biblical truths in a kid-friendly way is endless. Try to get into their world to make the meal you've prepared more edible for them.

Also, when you're using illustrations for kids, don't be afraid to get animated and be more expressive than normal. This may not come naturally to some preachers, but I want to encourage it nonetheless. Kids love seeing stories acted out, and getting into character for a few moments is a great way to make a passage come alive. The goal here isn't silliness for silliness' sake, but to capture their imagination and fill their mind with the greatness of God.

3. APPLICATIONS

The third and final menu item I want to encourage you to include is kid-specific applications. I assume a key part of your sermon each week is thoughtfully helping your congregation apply the text to their lives. As you do that, consider including a couple of points of application for the kids.

One of the most effective ways to teach kids they aren't spectators at church is by speaking directly to them about how they should live in light of what the Bible says. Consider the various commands we encounter in Scripture—commands like do not fear, put off anger, walk by faith, hope in God, and speak the truth in love, among others. Then think of the types of situations that arise in life in which kids can obey these commands.

Kids, notice what this passage teaches us. It teaches us that there is a connection between faith and being a peacemaker. Those who walk by faith will want to be peacemakers; they will want to give up their rights for the sake of unity. Does that describe you?

Would your parents say you're a peacemaker? Do you look for ways to make peace with your siblings, or do you look for ways to get what you want? Would your siblings say that you're the type of person who willingly gives up your rights for their sake, or do you always take for yourself the best seat, the best food, the best controller, the best clothing?

Just a little bit of application goes a long way.

And when it comes to application, you'll again want to consider the different ages of the kids in your congregation. Application for elementary schoolers will be different than application for teenagers. You can speak to teenagers in much the same way you speak to adults; however, I'd still encourage addressing them as a group so they realize you've prepared part of the meal for them.

You can talk with teens about the idols of the world like self-expression, popularity, and power; you can help them think through cultural issues related to gender or race; you can help them wrestle with difficult concepts like the Trinity, God's will, or eternal judgment. Some of the most fruitful and encouraging conversations I've had after church have been with teenagers who want to think more about how to apply the sermon to their lives.

CONCLUSION

We want our kids to know that the church is for them, Jesus is for them, and eternal life is for them, so let's speak to them in our sermons. Consider adding these items to your kids menu, and in time, you'll find a growing appetite among the kids.

John Joseph is the pastor of Cheverly Baptist Church in Cheverly, Maryland.

Children's Ministry Is NOT the Church

Nathan Loudin

Did you and your children join the church for worship last Sunday? It's possible you were both at the same address, but you gathered *with* the church while your children went to a ministry *of* the church.

Churches often betray their own convictions about the church, confusing parents and children along the way. Putting children's ministry in its proper place is not only a matter of ecclesiological preference; it influences how we affirm the salvation of our children.

CHILDREN'S MINISTRY IS A CHURCH'S MISSION FIELD

Jonathan Leeman helpfully defines the local church this way:

(i)   a regular gathering or assembly of people
(ii) who mutually affirm one another as Christians
(iii) through preaching the gospel
(iv) and participating in baptism and the Lord's Supper.

Notice the church is not *merely* defined by those who gather for worship. Non-Christians and unaffirmed professors of Christ will be gathered there too. Rather, a church is made up of those affirmed in their faith who gather around the Word and ordinances.

Might there be children of varying ages counted in church? Sure. It depends on the church. However, it's best not to think of children's ministry as part of the church. Instead, think of it as a mission field.

This mission field lives in our members' homes and follows them when they gather for church. Our members try to reach this "people group" through family devotions, loving discipline, and godly example. The church labors alongside, partnering with parents to reach their children by teaching the Bible and modeling the love they see at home. In doing so, they disciple parents how to parent.

This means children's ministry staff and volunteers are like evangelists commissioned by the church to reach this young mission field. They are trained by the church, background checked, and sent out by the church—even if it's just down the hall—for the purpose of reaching the next generation with the gospel of Jesus Christ.

How should we think about children's ministry if it is a ministry of the church and not the church itself?

STRUCTURE CHILDREN'S MINISTRY TO DISTINGUISH IT FROM THE CHURCH

Do we help children when our churches attempt to organize a mock church service down the hall from the actual church?

Children's ministry should not seek to mimic the church gathered. It should distinguish itself as a ministry of the church and not the church gathered. We should not have a separate sanctuary, a separate worship team, and a separate offering for their own mission projects. That becomes their "church."

Instead, offer Bible stories, practice catechism and Scripture memory, sing songs, and take time to play games and eat snacks. This all helps to distinguish between the church and its ministry to children.

AFFIRMING FAITH AND UNITY ABOUT BAPTISM

During children's ministry, we should be careful not to affirm faith in a way that replaces the role of the local church. If a child professes faith, we should encourage them that their faith is well placed and that Jesus is trustworthy, but remember baptism is the church's formal affirmation of faith.

Children's ministers and volunteers should know their church's age of baptism and membership policy. Otherwise, parents or ministry leaders may tell children, "You're a Christian! Now the next step is for you to get baptized," only to hear the elders say, "We're actually very hesitant to baptize seven-year-olds." Such a situation brings frustration and embarrassment for parents and leaders, as well as discouragement and confusion to children. If baptism *is* the church's affirmation of a profession of faith, that should affect the way we encourage professions of faith in children's ministry.

Elders should teach their convictions on baptism and help shepherd the church toward unity. We should avoid calling for professions of faith, and we should certainly avoid telling the children's class, "Billy is a Christian now!" We would not expect other ministries, such as benevolence or building and grounds, to exercise this kind of authority or make these kinds of judgments. Children's ministry doesn't hold the keys to affirm faith and membership.

Communicate clearly with the church and parents about how to encourage a child's faith without replacing the church's role in affirming professions of faith.

OUR CHILDREN SHOULD GATHER WITH THE CHURCH

The longer our children are separated from the gathered church, the more they will confuse the church's ministry to them as the church itself. In whatever tone, urgency, or volume, parents tell their children each Sunday, "It's time to go to *church!*" And upon arriving at the church building, children are dropped off in the children's wing.

What is church to them? The children's ministry and its volunteers? Who is the pastor, and what does he do? What is baptism and the Lord's Supper? What does it sound like for the church to sing? In our churches, a child could easily be eight, ten, or, in some cases, even older before they ever see or hear the church gathered!

At that point, considering travel and sick days, you can start counting the number of gatherings with the church before they leave the home. Imagine being the child of a church member and having never seen the church gathered until you were 10 years old.

Churches should encourage families to bring their children to gather with the church as early as they can. Let them hear the whole church sing. Let them meet Steve the deacon and sit next to Chris the new member. Let them watch their parents and the whole church listen to the pastor's 40-minute sermon with fixed attention. Bring children to see the Lord's Supper (and, as a result, see the church distinguish between them and the church).

PERSEVERE, PASTOR

How many pastors have had families leave for children's ministry-related matters?

I have. I sent this article to a friend before I finished it, and the first thing he said was, "A family just left our church in part because we didn't have a separate worship service for children."

Pastors and church leaders, the church is the display of God's glory! We should encourage our families to bring their children to church sooner rather than later.

Nathan Loudin is the senior pastor of Milwood Baptist Church in Austin, Texas.

Why A Pastor Should Care About Children's Ministry

Ed Moore

"PARTY WATER"

I invented "Party Water." "Party Water" is just water, and the kids all know that. Nonetheless, I use it as a gimmick to advertise "Pastor Ed's After-School Kids Class."

For the past two decades, I've met every Tuesday during the school year at 4 p.m. in my office with the elementary school students of our church. The 90-minute event draws about 15 children each week. We eat unhealthy snacks, play dodgeball in the basement, learn vocabulary words like "soteriology," study a passage of Scripture, color a picture, drink "Party Water," and dismiss. It's a pretty simple operation, but it constantly ranks as my favorite ministry activity of the week.

I don't have any deep philosophical underpinnings that support my rationale for doing it. Their parents are members of our church. I am their pastor. They are souls that will spend eternity somewhere, and this is an opportunity to give them the gospel.

As I search my heart, I honestly don't have anything profound to say about the necessity of the senior pastor being involved in ministering directly to children like this. It's pretty simple. They are people who need the Word of God. My schedule allows me to do it, and I desire to do it. That's pretty much all there is to it. I'm aware that my contribution is merely a supplement to their overall spiritual education.

Their primary source for learning about God and his Word must come from home. With that foundational understanding of children's ministry in place, I stand ready to reinforce what their parents teach them on a daily basis.

I recall being deeply impacted as a child by the deep concern my pastor showed for my soul. Even though I was unconverted and disinterested in spiritual things, I knew my pastor was *invested* in my salvation. Like all children, I didn't fully appreciate his commitment to my spiritual well-being until many years later. God only knows what the children of North Shore Baptist Church will remember half a century from now about our after-school class. One cannot do ministry with a crystal ball.

The Lord has ordained his desired end for each of these young people. I pray that he, by his gospel, will save them. I also know that the same God who ordained the end has also ordained the means by which that end will be accomplished. As pastors, we are to employ the means of preaching the gospel, which is the power of God unto salvation. This we do on Sunday mornings in front of the entire congregation. But it's also something we can do throughout the week with people of all ages God brings into our path.

In Matthew 19:14, Jesus said to his disciples, "Let the little children come to me and do not hinder them, for to such belongs the Kingdom of heaven." Much can be said about what this verse does not mean.

Admittedly, it's a somewhat challenging verse to understand and apply. However, when all the faithful exegesis has been completed, there is no doubt that children were precious in his sight. And they remain precious.

As pastors, we must follow the command of our Chief Shepherd, the one who said, "See that you do not despise these little ones" (Matt. 18:10). He was, of course, referring to all believers as the "little ones," but this certainly includes little believers.

As our Lord entered the temple in Jerusalem on Palm Sunday, he accepted the praise of the children who cried out, "Hosanna to the Son of David!" Christ then defended their right to extol him as King by quoting David in Psalm 8: "Have you never read, 'Out of the mouth of infants and nursing babies you have prepared praise'?" (Matt. 21:15–16)

Jesus, in the days of his flesh, had an awareness of and a love for the little children. We should love the little children, too.

Perhaps your schedule doesn't allow you to hold a weekly after-school class. Perhaps your church is too big or too little to hold such a gathering. The time, venue, and format are flexible. What's important is that we as pastors intentionally make an effort to show concern for the little ones in our midst. This is not to say there's no place for a "Director of Children's Ministries" in a church. Thank God for those who have expertise and gifting in this area! They serve the Kingdom greatly.

It is to say, however, that we as pastors should never fall into the trap of thinking we are above caring for the souls of young children.

Your context is likely different than mine. You'll need to responsibly assess your availability. But regardless of your weekly calendar demands, I would urge you to prayerfully consider making a genuine effort to know, to love, to spend time with, and to give the gospel to the children in your church.

Also, should you opt to employ the "Party Water" refreshment option, I'll expect royalties lest you violate the trademark.

Ed Moore is the senior pastor of North Shore Baptist Church in Bayside, New York.

Why Parents Are the Primary Spiritual Caregivers of Their Children

Rhys Plant

I was 20 years old when I became a father. I was young, dumb, and woefully unprepared. When my wife and I took our son home, we sat down and looked at each other. A wave of mixed emotions passed over us: joy, bewilderment, and panic. We were overjoyed at God's gift of a healthy baby boy. We were a little surprised that they would send two twenty-year-olds home with a baby and no instruction manual. And we were panicking because it was starting to dawn on us that we were now responsible for a tiny human, a little image-bearer. As I've talked with parents over the years, most have admitted to having had similar experiences.

I once heard someone say that parents have been given the job of "shepherding their children toward eternity." I can't remember who said it, but I've never forgotten the words. So, how can the church prepare parents to care for their children's souls?

Let me suggest four ideas.

1. REJOICE IN NEW LIFE AND GROWING FAMILIES.

The Psalmist writes, "Behold, children are a heritage from the Lord, the fruit of the womb a reward. Like arrows in the hand of a warrior are the children of one's youth. Blessed is the man who fills his quiver with them!" (Ps. 127:3–5). Unfortunately, fewer people today understand the value of children. Couples have fewer kids, often because they see them as an inconvenience, not a gift. This should not be the case in our churches. We should rejoice in the gift of children. If parents feel like they're not welcome at church because of their family's size or their children's behavior, then a church will have a hard time equipping their parents with the tools they need to raise their kids. Our Lord said, "Let the little children come to me and do not hinder them" (Mt. 19:14); that should also characterize our church's attitude toward kids.

2. TEACH PARENTS WHAT THEY'VE BEEN CALLED TO.

In Deuteronomy 6, the Lord calls parents to pass down the instructions of the Torah to their children: "You shall teach them diligently to your children, and shall talk of them when you sit in your house, and when you walk by the way, and when you lie down, and when you rise" (Deut. 6:7). Similarly, in Ephesians 6:4, Paul exhorts fathers to not "stir up anger in your children but bring them up in the training and instruction of the Lord." The Bible is clear; parents must instruct their children in the Lord.

So how can churches help parents understand this responsibility? Well, it starts in the pulpit. Pastors, as you preach the Word, take opportunities to apply your text directly to parents. Suggest questions they can discuss around the dinner table with their children. Encourage them as they evangelize their children. In addition to your pulpit work, ensure that your church's programs are structured so families can engage in worship together.

Many churches unintentionally hinder parental involvement by over-programming. A family may roll up to church on a Sunday, walk in the door, and not see each other again until they leave. They don't sing together. They don't pray together. They don't hear God's Word read together. They don't observe the ordinances together. And they don't listen to the sermon together. As pastors, we should avoid this when possible.

Children benefit from singing and praying with their parents. They benefit from seeing baptism and people taking the Lord's Supper.

Eventually, they need to hear the same sermons as their parents—and probably earlier than you think.

We must do all we can to help parents care for their kids' souls. This means encouraging them to worship together and giving parents accessible avenues to engage.

3. TEACH PARENTS *HOW* TO DO WHAT THEY'VE BEEN CALLED TO DO.

After teaching them what to do, churches should equip parents on *how* to actually do it. Historically, catechisms have been used to teach children the things of God. Perhaps your church can suggest different catechisms to use at home. Perhaps you may provide outlines for parents to use for family devotions so that they don't feel overwhelmed by having to devise their own system.

If your church has a bookstall, don't forget to stock the shelves with books for both parents *and* kids. During children's Sunday School or even in the nursery, teach the children in your church songs they can easily sing at home.

4. SUPPORT PARENTS IN THEIR CALLING.

Most parents know that sometimes our kids listen to others better than they listen to us. This is why a culture of discipling is so crucial for a healthy church. It should be normal for young people to be discipled by people other than their parents.

A straightforward way to foster these sorts of relationships is to encourage single members in your church to attach themselves to a family or two. When this happens, a family gains an extra set of hands, and the single members benefit from seeing the parents love their kids well—not to mention all the hugs, high-fives, and personalized crafts!

Ultimately, the best support we can offer is prayer. Parents can't guarantee their child's salvation. They simply point to the cross and pray. Fellow members can join parents in pointing and praying. So, pray for the children in your church. Pray for the children in your church's staff and elders' meetings. Pray for them in your quiet time. Pastors, you must help the parents in your church grow in their care for their children's souls. Don't depend primarily on programs. Instead, equip the saints for the work of the ministry by helping parents disciple their children toward maturity.

Rhys Plant is married to Natalie, the father of 5, and the pastor of Jacqueline Stree Alliance Church in London, Ontario.

How to Select a Children's Curriculum

Mark Redfern

Before becoming a full-time pastor, I spent over a decade in education. I worked day-in and day-out to prepare understandable lessons for my students. I managed classroom conflicts. I worked alongside peers and parents. I stood up in front of people to instruct them. I walked alongside them in the ups and downs of a given school year. I pursued a master's degree in curriculum and instruction. In other words, I was preparing to be a pastor, and even to write this article.

God used that time to teach me a thing or two about how to both evaluate and implement curriculum effectively.

Here are five ways your church can fruitfully engage with the plethora of curricular options at our disposal.

1. CHOOSE A THEOLOGICALLY RICH CURRICULUM.

Don't skimp on theology when it comes to your church's curriculum for children. The ultimate goal is to help our children to know God. As Psalm 78:5–7 says:

> He established a testimony in Jacob and appointed a law in Israel, which he commanded our fathers to teach to their children, that the next generation might know them, the children yet unborn, and arise and tell them to their children, so that they should set their hope in God.

We want the children in our churches to "hope in God." That comes as fathers (and mothers and others) teach them "the law and the testimony." The content of our curriculum must be uppermost in our priorities. We must ask: how does this curriculum encourage hope in God? Does it rely on the Word of God to foster such hope?

Don't settle for a shallow curriculum that fails to implant a growing knowledge of God as the center of its scope and sequence.

2. CHOOSE A GOSPEL-CENTERED CURRICULUM.

While "gospel-centrality" has become something of an evangelical buzzword, don't allow its overuse to dissuade you from its importance. Curriculum must not only be evaluated for *what* it is teaching, but *how* it aims to accomplish its goal.

While character formation is important, it must not be presented in a moralistic framework. Jesus taught us that the Bible is about himself (John 5:39, Luke 24). Therefore, look for a curriculum that's not only gospel competent, but also infused with a gospel climate. In other words, good curriculum draws the attention of children back (again and again, from every genre of Scripture) to the glory of God in the face of Jesus Christ.

3. CHOOSE AN INSTRUCTIONALLY DIVERSE CURRICULUM.

Not all children learn the same way. Back in my teaching days, I was encouraged to regularly remind myself, "The question is not, 'How smart are you?' The question is, 'How are you smart?'" This taught me to keep an eye out for the unique talents, gifts, and abilities present in my students and seek to instruct them in a way that—while developing areas of weakness—helped them to flourish in their strengths.

In the same way, we ought to look for children's curriculum that pays attention to these dynamics. Are all lessons presented in a one-dimensional way, only focusing on certain types of learners? Or is there an evident sensitivity to various learning styles, dispositions, and strengths?

And don't forget that the Bible has given us an "instruction manual for youth"; it's called the book of Proverbs. There we find Solomon utilizing lessons in observation, comparison, and metaphor to stimulate thinking and draw out application.

4. CHOOSE A PARENT-ENGAGING CURRICULUM.

As churches, we bear the responsibility for encouraging and strengthening the bonds between parents and their children. We don't want to undermine or usurp their role as the primary instructors of their children. Paul offers a wonderful balance in his letter to the Ephesians. He writes to both children and parents (Eph. 6:1–4), emphasizing to both parties their responsibilities to one another, all done in the context of the local church.

What do we learn from this? As pastors (and churches) our job is to come alongside both children and parents to equip both to live out their calling toward each other. We should seek curriculum that strengthens this obligation. The curriculum we choose would do well to have a "parental" component to it, whereby children and parents utilize lessons outside of the classroom. When used this way, curriculum can be a meaningful discipleship tool that reverberates beyond the Sunday School lesson.

From there, bring it up in prayer meetings. Periodically remind parents to engage their children about what they are learning.

5. Choose a habit-forming curriculum.

Repetition is a key to learning. Both our biblical and Reformed forebears knew this. Therefore, catechesis featured prominently in their educational approach. We would do well to choose a curriculum that is acquainted with these well-worn paths.

Ensure your curriculum has a category for the value of repetition, memorization, and catechesis. Curriculum must be not only engaging *in the moment*, but more importantly, *habit-forming* by inculcating songs, Scripture memory, and catechism questions so that lessons become lodged in the heart.

CONCLUSION

Ultimately, we depend on the Lord to "build the house" as we work with children (Ps. 127). But even so, may the Lord make us "wise builders" (1 Cor. 3) who seek to build *with the grain of Scripture* through theologically rich and gospel-centered content and *with the grain of children* through diverse instruction, parental engagement, and habit formation.[6]

Mark Redfern is a pastor of Heritage Baptist Church in Owensboro, KY.

---

6   Deepak Reju and Marty Machowski's book *Build on Jesus* is a great place to start. As for specific curricula, from my observation, three that accomplish the five aforementioned marks (and I'm sure there are more) are: The Gospel Project, Truth78, and Praise Factory.

Paul the Youth Pastor

Sam Emadi and Mark Redfern

THREE LESSONS ON YOUTH AND FAMILY MINISTRIES FROM EPHESIANS 6:1-4

Did you know that Paul was a youth pastor?

Don't believe me? Take a look at Ephesians 6:1–4:

> Children, obey your parents in the Lord, for this is right. "Honor your father and mother" (this is the first commandment with a promise), "that it may go well with you and that you may live long in the land." Fathers, do not provoke your children to anger, but bring them up in the discipline and instruction of the Lord.

Paul may not have an Xbox and a copy of Rock Band, but he's certainly doing the most basic job of a youth pastor: teaching "children" the Bible.

In fact, a closer look at "Paul the Youth Pastor" reveals several important principles we might apply in our churches as we seek to pastor children, youth, and families.

PARENTS, ESPECIALLY FATHERS, ARE THE PRIMARY SPIRITUAL LEADERS OF THEIR CHILDREN.

Compare verses 1 and 4:

- Verse 1—Children, obey your parents.
- Verse 4—Fathers, do not provoke your children to anger, but bring them up in the discipline and instruction of the Lord.

The primary, though not exclusive, sphere for discipling young people is the home. God holds parents responsible for training their children. Of course, Paul isn't suggesting that the church doesn't play any role in evangelizing and discipling children. After all, in this very passage "Paul the Youth Pastor" addresses children in the church with the Word of God and applies it to their lives (6:1–3). But by comparing verses 1 and 4, it's easy to see that Paul's ministry aims to strengthen the relationship between parents and children. Children are directed to obey their parents, and parents are told to disciple their children in the ways of the Lord.

Paul's emphasis on parents discipling their children challenges the overly common practice of *isolated* children's and youth ministries. Isolated ministries segregate children and youth from most of the life of the church. In these types of ministries, the church offers young people a version of seemingly everything: youth rooms, youth conferences, youth worship, youth groups, youth evangelism teams, youth mission trips, youth services. This isolationist model of ministry often unintentionally reinforces one of the chief lies our culture tries to peddle to young people: they don't need their parents.

But Jesus died to change all of that. In Christ's kingdom, the hearts of the fathers are turned toward their children and the hearts of the children turn back to the fathers (Mal. 4:6). In fact, one evidence of conversion in parents is that they have a heart for their children, and one evidence of conversion in children is a turning of their hearts toward their parents.

Ministries to young people should aid the work of evangelism and discipling that many Christian parents are already doing. A healthy children's or youth ministry will understand itself as a supplement.

Of course, some students who regularly attend your church may not have Christian parents, which is all the more reason to cultivate youth ministries that develop relationships between the youth and adult members of the church. These young people need spiritual mothers and fathers (Mark 10:29–31) which can only be found in the fellowship of God's people.

PASTORS SHOULD EQUIP PARENTS TO SHEPHERD THEIR CHILDREN

Paul simultaneously tells parents to disciple their children and equips them for the task. He pastors the fathers (and by implication the mothers) in the church: "Fathers, do not provoke your children to anger, but bring them up in the discipline and instruction of the Lord" (v. 4).

A healthy ministry to children and youth will occur not as you focus on them, but as you focus on equipping parents for the work of parenting. Your church may equip parents through Sunday School classes on parenting, family-equipping seminars, or any number of other discipling opportunities. Remember the best way to equip parents in your church is through the ordinary means of grace, the regular preaching of the Word, and by upholding faithful Christians (particularly the elders) as models of godly parenting.

CHURCHES SHOULD TEACH THE WORD OF GOD DIRECTLY TO CHILDREN

Parents may be the primary disciplers of their children, but that doesn't stop Paul the Youth Pastor from inserting himself into the lives of these Ephesian children (Eph. 6:1–3). Isolationist children's and youth ministries may be a problem, but also is the notion that churches should eliminate all age-segregated Bible instruction. The church still has a role to play—a supplementary one, but a significant one, nonetheless.

In this passage, Paul models how the church can directly minister to children and youth: teach them the Bible. He quotes Exodus 20:12, explains the text, and then applies it to their lives. It is entirely appropriate for pastors and members to teach children the Word of God directly as long as we keep in mind that the ultimate goal is to assist parents in their primary discipling responsibilities.

In short, what do we learn from Paul the Youth Pastor? Paul teaches kids the Bible and applies it to their lives, teaches in a way that leads children back to the authority of their parents, and equips parents to effectively disciple their children. Of course, this passage doesn't give us a comprehensive picture of how the church should minister to young people, but it's an instructive place to start.

Mark Redfern is a pastor of Heritage Baptist Church in Owensboro, KY.

Sam Emadi is senior pastor at Hunsinger Lane Baptist Church in Louisville, KY.

5 Steps for Preventing Abuse in Children's Ministry

Chad Holmgren

n what follows, I will offer five steps for preventing abuse in children's ministry. I offer them as a pastor whose primary area of influence is children's ministry. If you are a pastor thinking through this issue for the first time or a church planter starting a new children's ministry, my hope is to provide some direction and stimulate further thought. Before providing specific steps, however, I want to mention two of the many reasons why taking steps to prevent abuse should be a priority for pastors and children's ministries.

TAKING ABUSE PREVENTION SERIOUSLY

Taking steps to prevent abuse in children's ministry should be a priority because it's biblical. God places a high value on children. Scripture tells us that children are created in the image of God (Gen. 1:27), that children are a gift from God (Psalm 127:3), and that Jesus values children (Matt. 18:10).

The Bible instructs God's people to care for those who are vulnerable (James 1:27). Additionally, the Bible refers to pastors as shepherds (1 Pet. 5:2), and part of the responsibility of a shepherd is protection. In the context of a local church, there are those who can do great harm through false teaching and immoral behavior (1 Pet. 2:1–3). Wolves come in all shapes and sizes.

Taking steps to prevent abuse should also be a priority because it's wise, loving, and just. Tragically, in a world broken by sin, children are often victims of abuse. Statistics reveal that one in four girls and one in seven boys in the United States experienced sexual abuse in the last year.[7] The true numbers are almost certainly higher as many abuse cases are unreported.

Given the prevalence of child abuse in our society, a church should never assume abuse could not happen in its children's ministry. Wisdom, in light of the statistics, necessitates that churches take steps to prevent it. Here are five steps for preventing abuse in children's ministry:

1. PRIORITIZE CHURCH MEMBERSHIP

Church membership is not only biblical; it's practical. This is especially true when it comes to preventing abuse in children's ministry. In our church, we require that any adult who works with children is a member of our church and has attended for at least six months. This provides us with the opportunity to get to know our volunteers.

By the time an individual is asked or requests to serve in children's ministry, that individual has attended membership class, completed a membership interview, been recommended for membership by the elders, and been voted on by the congregation. Prioritizing church membership allows a congregation to develop a familiar relationship with individuals before entrusting those individuals to care for children.

2. SCREEN CHILDREN'S MINISTRY WORKERS

Establishing a screening process is a critical step in preventing abuse. Background checks are important but not nearly enough. The majority of sexual abuse cases are not reported. This means that in many cases of abuse no criminal record will exist for a perpetrator. Therefore, a thorough screening process will also include measures such as reference checks, interviews, and requiring an individual to complete an application before serving.

Prioritizing church membership and a thorough screening process are important steps. However, statistics suggest that up to 90 percent of children who are abused know their abusers.[8] Furthermore, sexu-

---

7   Centers for Disease Control and Prevention, https://www.cdc.gov/violenceprevention/childabuseandneglect/fastfact.html
8   Evangelical Counsel for Abuse Prevention, https://ecap.net/

al abusers groom children, leaders, and church communities in an attempt to establish trusting relationships. For this reason, additional steps are necessary.

3. IMPLEMENT A CHILD PROTECTION POLICY (CPP)

Perhaps the most important step to take in preventing abuse is to implement a Child Protection Policy. A CPP establishes specific policies and procedures that seek to safeguard a children's ministry from abuse. Think of a CPP like a high fence that is used to keep out those who would seek to harm a child. One key aspect of a CPP is to put in place a "Two Person Rule." A "Two Person Rule" requires that those who work with children are never in a situation where they are isolated and alone with a child.

A good CPP will also take into consideration both *power predators* and *persuasion predators.*[9] Power predators seek to take children by force. Persuasion predators seek access to children by gaining the trust of children, parents, and a church community through a grooming process. Persuasion predators will then leverage that trust to create opportunities to abuse children. While protecting against power predators is a concern, persuasion predators pose the greatest risk in children's ministry.[10] There are many resources available to help churches develop a robust Child Protection Policy. I will list a few helpful resources at the end of this article.

4. TRAIN AND EQUIP CHILDREN'S MINISTRY WORKERS

A CPP is beneficial only to the extent that it is known and followed. Children's ministry workers must know what policies and procedures are in place and why. Those who work with children should be able to recognize signs of abuse and be familiar with the grooming techniques used by predators. Children's ministry workers should also be informed about how to respond to suspected abuse cases.

---

9   Gavin de Becker, as cited by Deepak Reju in On Guard: Preventing Abuse at Church, 26
10   Ministry Safe, https://ministrysafe.com/the-risk/

Abuse prevention training can take place in many different formats. At our church we host an annual training for our children's ministry workers. We serve dinner, pray for children and families, and spend a large block of time reviewing our policies and procedures together. We require all new children's ministry workers to read through our CPP manual and consent to follow our policies. I make it a point to highlight specific children's ministry policies in my regular email correspondence with our volunteers. Abuse awareness training is also part of our approval process for children's ministry workers.

5. SEEK THE WISDOM OF OTHERS

The process of taking steps to prevent abuse in children's ministry can seem daunting. One easy step is to seek the wisdom of others. Thankfully, there are those who have thought through the issue at great length and have written on the topic. One helpful resource is Deepak Reju's book *On Guard: Preventing Child Abuse at Church*. *On Guard* is thorough and comprehensive. It's not only helpful in outlining the problem of abuse but also in offering practical strategies to protect against it.

Pastors and those who lead children's ministries can also benefit by connecting with other churches to find out how the issue is addressed in different settings. Organizations such as *Ministry Safe* and the *Evangelical Counsel for Abuse Prevention* are also great resources. The value of being informed and enlisting the help of others cannot be overstated.

CONCLUSION

The steps listed above should be viewed as a starting point. There's more that could be said on the subject of abuse prevention, especially regarding child protection policies. Ultimately, the greatest way we can care for children is by pointing them to Christ. Taking steps to prevent abuse creates a children's ministry environment where that is possible.

Therefore, we should view abuse prevention not only as a matter of safety, but of discipling the next generation. A children's ministry that thinks carefully about discipling the next generation must also think carefully about how to protect the children entrusted to its care.

Chad Holmgren is the Associate Pastor of Family & Children's Ministries and is the director of "In the Light" children's ministry. He, his wife Sarah, and their three kids enjoy getting together with other Cornerstone families, doing a variety of outdoor activities, and meeting new people.

Risks and Benefits of Age-Specific Ministry

Jason Seville

"**A**ll my guys want to do is play video games. I need to figure out how to get them off the couch and engaged in discipleship and ministry."

This lament, voiced by the youth pastor with whom I shared a seminary carpool back in 2009, would have been unremarkable in most situations. His frustration was representative of a myriad of youth workers over the last several decades.

But as we crept along on the construction-laden Texas interstate that early fall morning, two other realities forged with his complaint to create something of a *eureka* moment for me. First, during seminary I was serving as the associate director to the senior adult ministry at our church. Second, I had just read a news story the day before about how big box stores were having a hard time keeping Nintendo Wii gaming consoles on the shelves due to the high demand at senior living facilities.

"Wait a minute," I interjected. "This might be crazy, but do you think you could get your junior high kids to come play Wii with my senior adults?"

Fast forward through some brainstorming sessions, and our church's teens were doing nursing home and assisted living visitations, bonding over virtual bowling alleys and tennis courts with men and women who were sometimes 80 years their senior.

At its height, we hosted several Wii bowling tournaments in our church's Fellowship Hall. We'd have eight to ten "lanes" projected on the walls, whiteboards with Senior Adult vs. Junior High brackets, and prizes for the winners. Each ministry coached their demographic on what kinds of conversations would be edifying and encouraging to have.

"Hey Hailey, see the lady in the red sweater? She was a young girl during the Great Depression. You should ask her what that was like and how she saw God's hand of provision."

"Mr. Benton, you should be sure to introduce yourself to Taylor. Knowing your story, he reminds me of what I bet you were like at his age. Ask him what it's like trying to live as a Christian at his school."

Reflecting on that season of ministry, I'm freshly reminded of the two sides of the age-specific ministry coin. On one hand, the junior high and senior high ministries were incredibly fruitful in their own right (not to mention other age-segregated ministries in between). The ability to hone in on age-specific needs and opportunities served everyone in a personal and powerful way.

On the other hand, the combined events were reminders that there are many riches to be discovered with cross-generational ministry. There is a massive benefit to an integrated ministry approach that unleashes the saints to do the work of ministry with *everyone* in the church, rather than a small segment of it. We all have much to learn from—and much to offer—brothers and sisters who are in different seasons of life.

Let's reflect a bit more on the pros and cons of ministry which is divided by "age and stage."

RISKS & REWARDS OF AGE-SPECIFIC MINISTRY

The initial impulse is to make a list of the potential benefits of such ministry followed by a separate list of the potential deficits (or vice versa). However, I think it might be helpful to take a categorical approach because the pros and cons are linked together around various aspects of ministry. Consider the following six areas to weigh the risks and rewards of demographical ministry.

1. The comfort of community.

Positively, age-segregated ministry is more comfortable. We're with people who get our jokes, understand our issues, and use all the same cultural references.

Negatively, age-segregated ministry is more comfortable. Yes, you read that correctly. The pro can also be the con. When one considers biblical community, it doesn't seem like comfort was of prime importance. Perhaps pushing people out of their comfort zone is what we need most.

2. The gaps in discipleship.

A benefit of age-specific ministry is that it helps us think well about huge realities staring us in the face. College students can help each other think well about the pressures of course loads and what to do post-graduation. The young singles Bible study can encourage each other regarding the stewardship of their specific season.

At the same time, if we're not careful, we'll typecast everyone in our church. We'll foolishly proceed as if our teens don't need to consider the brevity of life along with our senior adults or that our senior adults don't need the same encouragements toward discipling children as our young marrieds do.

3. The struggle with sin.

Similar to the discipleship consideration, pigeonholing takes place when it comes to our battle against sin. Helping the 25-year-old deal with lust, the 45-year-old grapple with greed, and the 65-year-old face anxiety is a good and needed ministry. And an age-specific approach can aid us in dealing with sins that tend to pop up more prominently in specific seasons.

However, anyone who's spent any length of time in intentional ministry has had their categories shattered on this front. It may be that the 65-year-old is struggling with lust, the 25-year-old with greed, and the 45-year-old with lust, greed, and anxiety.

4. The witness to the world.

One of the great things about age-specific ministry is how attractive it is to outsiders. It's easy for someone to come to an event—be it youth or college or young adults—and see folks who look and dress and talk just like them. It's attractional, and that's not a bad thing in and of itself.

But there is the danger of attracting people to one segment of the church when the Christian life is to be lived out across all segments of the body. Additionally, the segregated approach misses out on the beautiful opportunity to unveil a "compelling community" that is diverse but united around a common love for Jesus.

5. The health of the family.

By "family," I have both the biological and church family in mind. It's the same consideration. On one hand, age-segregated ministry can serve by offering truly edifying events, instruction, and fellowship for our kids at various stages of development.

However, those same activities can pull our kids away from the family and the larger church gathering. This doesn't mean we ought to cancel the youth group; it just means we need to consider the timing and frequency of any such events.

6. The development of leaders.

The hyper-focused ministry that takes place within narrow demographics will allow our leaders to develop a sharp skill set in that area of ministry. Youth leaders can hold an attractional event with the best of them. No one can touch the college ministry when it comes to contact evangelism. Young adult pastors can officiate a wedding with a minute's notice.

You get the point. But very often, our youth pastors aren't prepared to preach a funeral. Our children's ministry leaders don't feel equipped to walk with a couple in pre-marital counseling. Our senior adult pastor has to reach way back in his training to coordinate an evangelistic outreach. If we're not careful, laser focus can become tunnel vision, and our leaders' growth will be stunted.

NOT MUTUALLY EXCLUSIVE

We could go on and on, and maybe it would be a healthy mental exercise for you to think about your church and how age separations—or lack thereof—either help or hurt any given aspect of ministry.

But if I may say one final word, it's that this doesn't have to be an *either/or.*

Your church may provide a youth group but do so at a time and with a frequency that doesn't constantly separate the children from the congregation. You may decide to provide age-specific Sunday School classes but do it occasionally rather than as the regular diet of the church. You can have a college ministry but make intentional decisions to connect them with families in the church. You can provide events for senior adults but ensure that your small group structure integrates generations in a way that has everyone rubbing elbows and learning from one another.

Praise God for the beautiful diversity in the local church! May we faithfully consider how to leverage "age and stage" for gospel purposes while avoiding the prevalent pitfalls. May the Lord give much grace.

Jason Seville (ThM) lives in Alexandria, VA with his wife and four daughters, where he serves as an elder at Del Ray Baptist Church. You can follow him on Twitter at @ jasoncseville.

How to Redeem Your Singles Ministry

John Lee

Being single in the church can seem like a "waiting room" for those who have entered adulthood but haven't found a spouse. For those who haven't figured out their life yet, *welcome to singleness*.

But the singles in your church are gifts, not consolation prizes. How do you care for the singles of your church without them feeling like they're attending a Christian speed-dating event?

I don't know *what* your church does, whether it's singles ministry or events. But many churches would be helped by watching *how* you care for singles, not just what you do for them.

1. WATCH YOUR TONE

How would you preach this to your singles? In 1 Corinthians 7:8–9, Paul, a single man, says, "I say to the unmarried and to widows: It is good for them if they remain as I am. But if they do not have self-control, they should marry, since it is better to marry than to burn with desire."

Usually, we're quick to jump to the latter half, that people who lack self-control should marry. That's true, but let's not skip verse 8. Paul's *preference* for singleness may not be shared by some singles, but his *perspective* is that singleness itself is good.

Even more, look at *whom* Paul addresses. Paul's audience isn't limited to those who have a supernatural ability for asexuality, but to the unmarried and widows. He views singleness as so good, he's even willing to encourage widows—who have been married before—to remain single! It's not that singleness is good for a select few, but singleness *itself* is good. It is good to remain single.

What are the unique advantages of singleness? What are the ways you've seen singleness practiced in your church well? How do singles fit into the life of your church?

How you answer these questions will color the way you speak about singleness to your church. Singleness is not a problem to be fixed, but a gift to be celebrated.

Would your members say the *tone* with which you talk about singleness affirms its goodness?

The *way* we talk about singleness communicates how we *value* singleness. A husband who consistently speaks disparagingly of his wife may claim to love her, but he functionally dismantles her. A husband who encourages his wife and celebrates her gifts builds her up. In the same way, we have an opportunity to build up singles with our tone. Cherish your singles through your speech.[11]

2. MAKE GODLINESS YOUR PRIMARY AIM

What's the end goal for singles in your church?

If we make our primary aim marriage, we miss the mark. For one, some singles in your church have already been married. Some who have same-sex attraction may not see biblical marriage as an option. Others will desire marriage for decades and not be married. If marriage is the destination, they will be stuck on a perpetual Ferris wheel of dating tutorials, marriage advice, and calls to "move on" from adolescence.

Now, marriage is a wonderful gift, like so many other good gifts that God gives. But our singles ministry should aim at godliness. Would Paul, a single man, be able to benefit from your singles ministry? Would Jesus?

Your ministry will be shaped by its goals. So aim for godliness.

That may mean focusing less on where someone may desire to be in the future and focusing on where they are now. Help your singles be captivated by Christ.

---

11 I'm deeply grateful for so many pastors who have encouraged and built me up in my singleness. Thank you!

Help them practice godly contentment that acknowledges the difficulties of singleness, sees the blessings of singleness, and trusts Jesus in *every* circumstance, not *just for* a future marriage. Help your singles leverage their undivided attention to soak in God's Word, think deeply about Christ, and prioritize prayer. Help them leverage their flexibility and freedom to serve other members in the church.

One way I do this is by using our church covenant. I regularly sit down with single members of my congregation, read through the church covenant, and ask, "How can you obey this church covenant in ways that married members can't?" Empower your singles by giving them a vision of a godly single life now.

3. INTEGRATE YOUR SINGLES

Jesus promises in Mark 10:

> Truly I tell you … there is no one who has left house or brothers or sisters or mother or father or children or fields for my sake and for the sake of the gospel, who will not receive a hundred times more, now at this time—houses, brothers and sisters, mothers and children, and fields, with persecutions—and eternal life in the age to come. (Mark 10:29–30)

Jesus' promise of family isn't just for the new heavens and earth, but for today. When we integrate singles into the family life of the church, we display the fulfillment of Christ's promise.

There are unique challenges and blessings to singleness that deserve special attention. But if your singles ministry is primarily oriented around young single folks discipling and sharing life with other young single folks, then you may be showing your singles a deficient view of a flourishing single life. Dividing a body by demographic diminishes its unity found in the gospel.

I've been blessed by so many church members who have welcomed me into their lives, married saints who have invited me into delights and conflicts, and families who have shared their chaotic and cherished moments. I'm happily an adopted son and uncle, dozens of times over. The privilege of seeing the mystery of the gospel displayed in married life is a grace to me. I *need* these families in my life.

Your married members also need singles in their lives—to provide perspective that married members no longer have. Singles serve as physical reminders that in heaven, we will "neither marry nor [be] given in marriage" (Matt. 22:30). Children who spend time with flourishing singles get to see satisfaction greater than finding a spouse who "completes them." Married couples get to see faith in the sufficiency of Christ. As Sam Allberry says, "If marriage shows us the shape of the gospel, singleness shows us its sufficiency."[12]

Lead your church in praying that married members would share life with fellow single members. Encourage married members to dismantle the need to show an ideal home life. Encourage single members to go beyond their comfort zone and reach out to married members (even inviting families into *their* home!).

Mark Dever has remarked that his own church has experienced the health and growth it has in part because of the many singles. They're available for discipling and other good works in a way that married folks can't always be.

Singles in your church aren't in spiritual limbo, stuck in a waiting room until they graduate into marriage. Rather, they've received a unique gift from God for this season to serve and love the Lord. Help them to see that their single life for Jesus is absolutely worth it.

John Lee is a pastor of Bethany Baptist Church in Bellflower, CA. You can follow him on Twitter @JohnHBLee or email him at hhjohnlee@gmail.com.

---

12 https://www.thegospelcoalition.org/article/how-celibacy-can-fulfill-your-sexuality/

Raising the Cane: Refreshing Ministry to Senior Saints

Will Pareja

You're probably reading this because members of your flock are aging. They need shepherding, but you're not exactly sure how to proceed. After all, you may be young enough to be their child— or their grandchild!

This has been the situation in the church I've pastored for the last 10 years. Thankfully, Scripture is profitable for teaching us how to shepherd our senior sheep. When old Paul wrote to young Timothy about how the church should behave, embedded in his instruction were principles for engaging older members (1 Tim. 3:15; 5:1ff).

PRINCIPLES FOR SENIORS MINISTRY

It's possible for any ministry of the church to lose its way and become a silo, especially the senior saints' ministry. They have faithfully served for years and outlasted many pastors, so messing with their ministry might feel like raising your hand against the Lord's anointed. They might even start raising cane!

Yet many elderly church members are sincerely open to the next generation of servant leaders. So, take courage. Especially in a church that has more grayheads than towheads, it's necessary not only to plan for the church's future but also not to neglect the ones who maintained it long before you got there—even if you introduce a different ministry philosophy.

Whether you're a pastor or a deacon responsible for the care of senior saints, here are some suggestions on refreshing them in Christ:

1. Build trust.

Trust is a necessary currency in any relationship, and don't expect to be handed it easily just because you're in a church. Remember: seniors have a lot of history before you came into their lives. You may be ready to pastor them, but they may not be eager for you to pastor them. Tread confidently, but also gently and compassionately.

Ask them lots of general questions. Over time, it doesn't matter if they've told you the same story over again. Though senior saints don't have much to hide, this doesn't mean they'll volunteer their whole life story in a couple of conversations. These elderly souls are worth getting to know because the Jesus in them is worth honoring. Be patient.

In other words, spend time with them. Go to their homes—and not just when they're sick. Some of you won't struggle with this. But for the over-eager shepherds out there, understand that your overtures of care will not always be welcome. Give them space and keep your ear ready for them. Seek to learn. Squeeze what wisdom you can. Though not all senior saints are equally spiritually mature, you'd be surprised what you could still learn from them.

One principle has helped me throughout the past decade. RSBW: Respectfully show a better way. I taped this acronym to my desk in the early years and still remind myself of it. You'll likely find yourself at odds with those who resist your ideas for change. Wisdom is needed to navigate some of the unhealthy aspects of a senior saints' ministry. But respect is also. You must always take the high road of respect, even if you're treated disrespectfully. That's part of the love debt— "respect to whom respect is owed" (Rom. 13:7).

2. Serve them; don't sideline them.

Especially as the church gets younger, be deliberate about contacting the senior saints. Reach out to them, not just with your thumbs, but also with the good old-fashioned telephone—or even, believe it or not, paper, ink, and pen.

Members who've served the church for a long time become tired. They've shown up faithfully even when others flaked, but they're no longer able to serve like they used to. Assure them of God's love and the church's appreciation. It's imperative that you thank and honor them—frequently. Do so genuinely, personally, and publicly. Tell them the church wouldn't be where it is today without their faithfulness yesterday.

Some elderly saints aren't as mobile or don't have family close by. They have practical needs like a ride to the doctor or changing a light bulb in their house. Introduce them to younger people in the church and encourage those younger people to meet those needs. Intergenerational bonding between members during the week will make elderly church members feel more cherished and connected during gathered worship.

3. Train them.

Sadly, some senior saints weren't thoroughly discipled earlier in life or meaningfully deployed to disciple others. So, when younger people arrive at the church wanting to live out the intergenerational ideals of Titus 2:1–10, the older saints often feel like deer in headlights. Encourage the older saints to keep learning the Word in community. Don't take "it's hard to teach an old dog new tricks" for an answer. Gently and positively show them their potential to still influence younger saints with the vigor and vision of Caleb (Josh. 14:6–12), all while facing the realities of a declining body (Ecc. 12).

Aside from including the senior saints in the normal rhythms of church life, why not give them some special attention? One of the things I tried years ago was humorously entitled "Senior Sprinters." This was meant to encourage the older saints of our church to finish well. I knew then that *I* couldn't change them. So I borrowed from someone more credible than me—J.I. Packer. Over a period of four sessions, we went through his book *Finishing Our Course With Joy* (don't worry, it has big font). It was a lovely time and well-attended. Many of them felt loved, even during a period of church life full of some bitter tensions.

John wrote to the "fathers" (the older men) "because you know him who is from the beginning" (1 John 2:12–14). In the church, you don't just want people with the strength to go, go, go. Help the aging saints to recognize that the willingness of youthful energy needs to be combined with the experiential wisdom of saints who've aged well.

CONCLUSION: START WITH THE CRADLE

A church's ministries often span generations. So, from the cradle to the cane, ensure that everyone is being taught with the goal of presenting each person mature in Christ (Col. 1:28). While it's right to focus on the people you're actively serving, realize that what you do and whom you serve will hopefully outlast you and even be transplanted to other churches.

If you want a senior saints' ministry that's meaningfully aligned with God's mission for your church, then start early. Begin by training parents to catechize their children. Why? Because when these children grow up, they will faithfully follow Jesus. If that happens, then the next pastor(s) won't have to worry about throttling *or* jumpstarting a senior saints' ministry. Because the church will be full of senior saints who are the mature oaks of righteousness that every church needs.

Will Pareja is a pastor of Addison Street Community Church in Chicago, Illinois.

Our Main Goals for Youth Ministry: Teaching and Discipling Our Teens

Deepak Reju

What do we typically expect from youth ministry in the United States?

EXPECTATION #1: A YOUTH CULTURE THAT IS ATTRACTIONAL TO DRAW STUDENTS

The burning question is: how can we structure our youth group in order to maximize the number of students who come?

Let's offer lots of fun games. Add unhealthy food as a draw for hungry students—pizza, cupcakes, soda, ice cream. You're also taught from the Bible, but it's typically on the lighter side. The cynics tell us: "We dare not challenge teens with teaching that is substantial, deep, and theological. That's too much."

Some will supplement with sleepovers, camps, or retreats—all meant to draw the native teen out of his daily context to offer some relational bonding, more fun, and more teaching (again, typically on the lighter side).

EXPECTATION #2: A YOUTH CULTURE THAT IS A SEPARATE SUBCULTURE OF THE CHURCH

Some churches encourage, fund, and facilitate a separate youth culture, independent of the rest of the church. Maybe they offer a youth service, which runs at the same time as the main service. They provide options, like a theatre with different movies playing in different rooms. Parents attend the main church service, teens go to the youth meetings, and the younger kids enjoy children's church. Everyone gets their needs met, so everyone's happy.

Some churches won't go that far; they don't split everyone up or tailor the programming to meet each age group's needs. But even if we're all together in church, the youth still find ways to separate from the church body. I remember at a previous church watching the teenagers sitting together in the balcony, apart from the adults. They *always* sat as a group—a youth "church" within the larger church.

The youth group sitting separately stood out to me. It didn't bother me at the time, but it does now.

THE TRANSFORMATION OF CHBC'S YOUTH GROUP

When I arrived in DC in 2007, the youth group was small (3-8 kids). Amidst the high turnover of youth leaders, and the relatively small number of students, we made a humble effort to help the few kids. In 2014, Charles arrived. He had a lot of experience working with teenagers, so over the next few years, he reached out to teens and their parents and built relationships with them. Before my eyes, over the next few years, everything changed. By the time we hit 2019, we had 50 to 60 teens from multiple churches gathering once a week for teaching, games, and small groups.

Granted, 50 to 60 kids is small compared to many youth groups in suburban churches, but for a city church, it's fairly big. Families of high schoolers don't tend to stick around in the city but retreat to the suburbs for better schooling options.

Scott was the father of one of our teens. Unlike most parents who simply dropped off their kids, he came to our youth meeting. Before he committed his kids to our youth ministry, he wanted to check us out. His feedback was encouraging, and it's an illustration of our first goal for youth ministry—to build a program around solid, biblical teaching.

Scott, a four-star general in the Airforce, had seen several youth groups over the years. Most of those youth groups had a lot of fun and games, but weak teaching. So, he was delighted to see how substantial

Charles' teaching was to our teenagers—it was robust, theological, and embedded in the biblical text. It stood out.

We had youth retreats, good old-fashioned fun, and food to feed the kids (like many youth groups). But the centerpiece of our youth ministry was rich expositional teaching.

THE ELDERS' DIRECTIVE: BUILD A CULTURE OF DISCIPLING OUR TEENS

As the youth group quickly grew under Charles' leadership, I asked the elders of Capitol Hill Baptist Church (CHBC) to speak and give us some direction. I didn't want to get out ahead of their leadership. After all, Charles and I were both men under authority.

Over a series of meetings with the elder board, we discussed a variety of goals for youth ministry, brainstormed with subcommittees, and prayed for direction. One priority emerged: *foster a culture of discipling with the teenagers.* They wanted us to build a bridge from the rest of the church into the lives of our teenagers.

Most church subcultures exist as isolated islands—the married folk, the single folk, and the teenagers all hang out with their own kind, with little intermingling. Married folk invite singles over to babysit kids, but they wouldn't ask singles to join their family vacation. Single folk get together for fun and fellowship. Rarely do singles request married folk to attend. A few married or singles volunteer with the youth group, yet seldom would the rest of the church interact with those teenagers outside of the youth ministry. In a typical church, walls exist between these social groups. Little effort is made to cross over, apart from occasional conversations on Sundays after church.

The CHBC elders had built a culture of discipling that overcame many of these social barriers. Married and singles are invested in each other's lives—and by the grace of God, it's the normal way our church lives together. But our next step was to foster a culture where the church learned to disciple the teenagers. Apart from singles volunteering for youth ministry, or married folk asking teenagers to occasionally babysit, there was little interaction between the church body and teens.

When I use the term "culture of discipling," I mean *it is the personality of the church to disciple, evangelize, and shepherd the teenagers.* Think of it this way:

- It's not a formal program, like a youth ministry, but it's an inclination of many church members to deliberately invest in the teenagers of the church.
- Members don't have to sign up for anything or get permission to love the teens.
- It's normal for the members to take initiative to love the teenagers and do them spiritual good.

This culture is what the elders asked Charles and me to help build. If mark number one of a healthy youth ministry is *solid teaching*, then mark number two is a *culture of discipling*.

WHERE DO WE START? PRAYING TOGETHER AS A CHURCH

We're at the early stages of building this culture of discipling teens. It feels a bit like building the airplane while flying it. But the most important first step we've taken is to pray.

On Sunday nights, our church gathering focuses on praying together. Pastor Dever often shares a prayer request like: "Let's pray that we'll grow to be a church where we're committed to discipling our teenagers."

I've noticed an unexpected additional benefit when we take the time to pray. Mark is the primary preacher for our church. He's the primary culture shaper of our congregation. So, when Mark communicates a prayer request (whatever it is), it's not just a prayer request; it also creates an expectation.

At our Sunday night prayer meeting, Mark shares many requests related to discipling: "Let's pray that we would be a church who asks each other hard questions"; "...who will be invested in each other's lives"; "...who studies the Bible together." And now: "...who will disciple our teenagers."

When he states these things, he's encouraging us to ask for the Lord's help. But he's also saying: *This is how we should live as Christians. This is what we should strive for as a church.*

OUR PRIORITIES: TEACHING AND DISCIPLING

I've personally seen the benefit of youth ministry in the lives of my own children. I'm grateful both as a parent and a pastor for the teaching and for the members actively discipling my kids.

My hope is that in the years ahead, we'll communicate solid truths, destroy social barriers, and watch members pour into our teens. Pray with us that the Lord would see fit to grant us these things.

Deepak Reju is an associate pastor of Capitol Hill Baptist Church in Washington, D. C. He has a PhD in biblical counseling from the Southern Baptist Theological Seminary.

Small Groups: Thoroughfares, Not Cul-De-Sacs

Andy Johnson

For those who don't know, a cul-de-sac is a half-circular blip off a road that doesn't go anywhere. As a kid, my family and I lived on one, and I loved it. Without through-traffic, my sister and I could skate in the street and never worry about getting hit. Our cul-de-sac may not have been helpful for going somewhere, but it was comfortable.

I think that describes what many folks want out of their church's small groups—a small, manageable group of people that offers a refuge from the diversity and challenges of the larger church. Many churches want their small groups to be familiar and safe.

But do small groups have to be this way? Not necessarily. I believe we should treat small groups not as cul-de-sacs but as thoroughfares. You drive through them to get somewhere.

I realize folks like small groups for a variety of reasons. Some are evangelistic, while others function as seasonal Bible studies. Some focus on acute local needs, while others attend to specific sin issues. Yet sometimes groups are for fellowship and community, and that's my interest here—when churches employ small groups as community builders.

Community building is a fruitful but risky strategy for a church. They can encourage members but also morph into cul-de-sacs of complacency.

How? The very things that make them comfortable can also prevent members from striking out into the diversity of relationship opportunities available in the whole church. That's a significant danger.

As you think about the small group ministry in your church, pastor, your goal should be to avoid making them ends in themselves. Ask, how can you use the small groups to push people into the larger fellowship of the church? How can you use them as thoroughfares rather than as cul-de-sacs?

CUTTING UP FOOD SO YOU DON'T CHOKE

So why risk having these groups at all? Perhaps another analogy will help.

I love steak, especially with salt and a brush of butter. But if you drop a huge ribeye steak in front of me, I'm not going to swallow it in one bite. I'm going to cut it up, so I don't choke.

Many people consider intentionally loving the whole church like trying to down a ribeye in one bite. How do you even start? Small groups can be a "one bite at a time" solution. They help people take the first bite by helping them to build relationships with half-a-dozen people.

But—and this is the key—you don't want your members to stop there. I wouldn't take one smokey bite of steak, lay down my cutlery, and lean back satisfied. I take another bite.

Similarly, members shouldn't be satisfied with just the relationships in their small groups. They should lead folk to pursue other relationships as well.

THEOLOGICAL ISSUES

Theologically, a church and a small group aren't the same thing. The former is more important than the latter; it's prescribed in Scripture. Small groups are not. Therefore, they should be less central to our discipleship, even if we have great affection for them.

Jonathan Leeman has helpfully defined a local church as "a group of Christians who regularly gather in Christ's name to officially affirm and oversee one another's membership in Jesus Christ and his kingdom through gospel preaching and gospel ordinances." A small group isn't *that*, though it may exist to serve that central goal.

God means to be glorified in the diversity of his church, not the small group, especially when they're homogeneous. Notice what Paul writes to the church in Ephesus regarding their maturity in Christ: "From him the whole body, fitted and knit together by every supporting ligament, promotes the growth of the body for building itself up in love by the proper working of each individual part" (Eph. 4:16).

That's what we want, right? A church where every member is growing and helping others to grow so that the whole body—not just a small group—is built up in love.

SOCIAL AND STRUCTURAL ISSUES

Another issue to consider is the social dynamic that can turn small groups into cul-de-sacs rather than thoroughfares: we like to be with people who are like us.

No one wonders why groups of similarly-situated people—singles, college students, young parents, retirees, etc.—spend time together. No unbeliever observes groups like this and wonders how they could love each other. There's no gospel mystery there.

But what happens when a women's small group has a few single women, a young mom, a recent immigrant who speaks limited English, and an older widow? Maybe it meets weekly in a local coffee shop. They laugh, cry, hug, and pray. What will observers say then? They might wonder how such a group exists.

How do you get that kind of group? One way is to structure small groups according to church members' differences instead of their similarities. No doubt, practical issues of availability may limit you. Single women may need to meet after work, while moms with small kids may need to meet midday at the park. Nonetheless, pastors should try to create groups marked by differences that confound the world and commend the gospel.

Another challenge is that members may prioritize their small groups over the whole church. You know this is happening when small groups schedule their meetings during regular church gatherings, like the church's Sunday night prayer meeting. More commonly, it shows up when people don't think twice about missing church but hate skipping out on small group.

HELPING SMALL GROUPS BECOME THOROUGHFARES

What can you as a pastor do to help the church's small groups act less like cul-de-sacs and more like thoroughfares?

For starters, regularly add new members to small groups. You might also reassort small groups from time to time. If a group resists adding new folks, or boasts, "We've been together for five years," then you may have a cul-de-sac on your hands.

You also need to carefully select and train small group leaders. They don't need to be super Christians, but their maturity should show itself in their love for the church at large. Their love for people outside the group will help to foster this kind of love inside the group.

Reoccurring training is valuable, but new leader training is essential. This is where you should set out your vision of small groups as thoroughfares into the wider church community, not cul-de-sacs where folks can hole up with a few close friends. In fact, small group leaders should consider it one of their main goals: helping members serve others outside the group.

CONCLUSION

Even the clearest theology and the best pastoral efforts won't guarantee that groups resist the urge to become relational fortresses outfitted with a mote and a drawbridge. We all have to fight against the desire to keep life safe, familiar, and small.

Nevertheless, taking notice of the warnings above should help your small groups to become assets, especially to a larger or fast-growing congregation.

This is precisely why every small group meeting should afford some opportunity to focus on the Bible. Whether our groups center on a Bible study, a book about the Christian life, or a recent sermon, we're reminded that sharing Jesus in common makes our most defined differences look small.

The Word reminds us that we're united together because we're united to Christ. Even if that's all we have in common, it's enough, and it's glorious.

Andy Johnson is an associate pastor at Capitol Hill Baptist Church in Washington, DC.

How Small Groups Can Foster Church Unity... Or Fracture It

Dave Russell

L ong ago, at many times and in many ways, churches built their discipleship around Sunday School, evening services, and midweek Bible studies and prayer groups. But in these last days, it is more common to find small groups at the center of a church's ministry philosophy.

Local churches are free to organize additional assemblies outside of the main Lord's Day gathering, but it's important to consider how they can either foster church unity or fracture it. The apostle Paul exhorted the Ephesians to be "*eager* to maintain the unity of the Spirit in the bond of peace" (Eph. 4:3). Small groups have the potential to be a tool for maintaining church unity—when they are led wisely.

HOW SMALL GROUPS CAN FOSTER CHURCH UNITY

1. When they offer another context to spend time in the Word and prayer.

At their best, small groups help members to live out the principles of your church covenant. My local church's small group ministry aims at building up members through studying the Bible, discussing the sermon, or reading a Christian book.

Furthermore, the gatherings allow members to pray with one another about personal needs and the ministry of the church. Unity is strengthened as members pray for the regular preaching of God's Word, the elders, and needs in the congregation. Each member of a small group will have 2-3 times a month protected in their calendar to spend with others in the

Word and prayer. For members juggling busy schedules, this type of structure is useful for getting them into true fellowship consistently.

2. Small groups help members care for one another.

Small groups provide a context for members to build deeper relationships. And the deeper the relationships, the more members will encourage one another, confess sin, and seek spiritual help.

Practical needs often come up easily in small groups (birth of a child, sickness, financial hardship, etc.). When groups become aware of opportunities to care for members, that information can be passed on to elders for spiritual care or to deacons for practical needs. In this way, small groups are a tool that better connects members to one another and to church leaders.

3. Small groups help members form discipling relationships.

Small groups are a great place for discipling relationships to form. While discipling should happen outside of small groups, it naturally follows that discipling relationships will form where there is regularly scheduled investment in the spiritual lives of others.

Finding discipling relationships is often challenging for members, and small groups provide a context where those relationships form and grow organically. Then those connections create momentum for building relationships among the whole local church.

HOW SMALL GROUPS CAN FRACTURE UNITY

1. When They Take Away from the Main Gathering

At our church, we prioritize the gathering of the whole church. Small groups should never become a substitute for church attendance. If members begin to treat their small groups as the main place for teaching and transformation, the group ends up working against the teaching of the church rather than complementing it.

The ministry of a local church begins with the main gathering on the Lord's Day and works out from there to opportunities like Sunday evening services, education classes, and small groups. Each local church must decide what they prioritize outside of the main gathering, but those additional contexts should not leave the pews emptier on Sunday morning.

2. When They Are Viewed as the Primary Context for Relationships

Every member of a local church has covenanted with every other member of their church to live in fellowship together. Small groups may allow relationships to form quickly, but members must commit to building relationships broadly.

Our church doesn't want small groups to become insular. If members view their relationships in the church as being primarily contained in their small group, they fail to care for other covenant members. Small groups should be viewed as *a* context for relationships, not *the* context.

3. When They Divide Age and Life Stage

Members of the same age and life stage will naturally connect with one another. Church leaders don't need to spend as much time facilitating these types of relationships.

Small groups should do more than gather friends who already share common interests. By gathering older members with younger members, married members with single members, small groups become a tool to encourage discipling relationships among different demographics.

Dave Russell is the Senior Pastor of Oakhurst Baptist Church in Charlotte, North Carolina. You can follow him on Twitter at @DRussinQC.

Parachute, Not Parachute: Advantages and Disadvantages of Extra-Church Bible Studies and Fellowships

Sam Crites

'm a pastor who is the product of parachurch ministries.

I have a Master of Divinity degree from Southwestern Baptist Theological Seminary. I'm working on my PhD at the Southern Baptist Theological Seminary. Both my parents taught Precept Bible studies when I was growing up. As a student at Texas A&M University, I participated in Breakaway Ministries and served as a counselor at Impact Camp. As an adult, I taught Precept myself, I have served on the board of multiple parachurch ministries, and I graduated from Downline Ministries' Discipleship Institute. God has used parachurch ministries to shape me into the pastor I am today.

Over the last two years, as I prepared to plant our new church in College Station, my understanding and love for the local church have grown. This has made me reevaluate the roles that parachurch ministries have played in my spiritual formation, and left me asking the question, "Where was the church?"

This question hits at the heart of the tension between the church and the parachurch. But before we address that tension, let's ask a preliminary question: what is a parachurch organization? Here is a working definition: *any organization that is not a local church, that seeks to accomplish one aspect of the mission that Christ has given to the church.*

Here are a couple of important things to observe about this definition.

1. The church is essential, not the parachurch.

Christ has promised that he will establish the church, and the gates of hell will not prevail against it (Matt. 16:18). He has not promised to establish a parachurch ministry. The church is plan A, and there is not a plan B.

2. The parachurch is not a humanitarian organization.

The parachurch must be attempting to accomplish at least some part of the same ultimate mission of the church: discipling the nations for the glory of God (Matt. 28:18–20). One of the benefits of the parachurch is that it can specialize in different aspects of this goal. It can train pastors, send missionaries, teach the Bible, evangelize the lost, focus on niche demographics, and more. While a parachurch can engage in humanitarian efforts, what makes it a parachurch is that it performs those services toward the ultimate ends of the church.

THE TENSION BETWEEN PARTIES

The tension between the church and the parachurch can be seen in how the parachurch accomplishes its ministry. Some parachurches are healthier than others. On the healthy end of the spectrum, the parachurch conducts its ministry by serving the church. On the unhealthy end of the spectrum, the parachurch attempts to accomplish the mission of the church, unwittingly or not, by replacing or sidelining the church.

Every pastor reading this article can probably think of many parachurch organizations that exist somewhere along this spectrum. There are amazing, healthy parachurch organizations that serve the church well and stand in the gap where the church has massive blind spots. There are also parachurch organizations that unfortunately operate as if the church is *not* the means God has established to accomplish the Great Commission, but an obstacle in the way.

Unhealthy parachurch organizations create problems inside and outside the church. Inside the church, an unhealthy parachurch can teach church members to be lazy. When the church outsources its primary responsibilities, such as teaching the Bible, evangelizing the lost, training pastors, planting other churches, and sending missionaries, the members of the church can wrongly assume that the church can choose to opt-in to these tasks.

When a parachurch ministry is meeting certain needs, some may feel like there's no need to reinvent the wheel. Church members might reduce their obligation to writing checks to the experts. They may divert funds that would otherwise go to their local church to their favorite parachurch ministry and thereby rob the church of the financial resources and manpower necessary to fill the gap that the parachurch services.

The unhealthy parachurch can also create problems outside the church. Parachurch ministries tend to be seasonal or specialized, meaning they focus on a particular age group (college ministries, Christian camps, etc.) or they specialize in an area of ministry (inductive Bible study, pastoral training, etc.). This can create a distorted view of the Christian life.

Let me explain. The church is full of people who are struggling, people who are dying, people who are in different stages of maturity. The parachurch exists in a more controlled environment. Once a Christian leaves the season of life where the parachurch focuses, they may find it extremely difficult to transition to the local church.

The key to healthy parachurch ministry is to make sure its ultimate goal is to support and encourage healthy churches. I say its ultimate goal because parachurches naturally go through a life cycle. Often, parachurch ministries come into existence because the church is failing in some area. This can be good for them to do. More gospel opportunities exist than any local church with limited resources can engage. Therefore, the parachurch is a gift to the church.

The problems arise if the parachurch forgets that they can't replace the church. The parachurch should not look with disdain on the church, but transition to resource and train the church to see and fill the gap in which it has failed. The life cycle of the parachurch should begin with filling the gap the church has missed, raising awareness in the church, and then serving the church by resourcing and platforming the church to meet the need that has been identified.

TAKEAWAYS

As this is an article to pastors, not parachurch directors, let me leave you with some takeaways.

First, teach your people to love the local church. The church is flawed, but it is the only institution in God's kingdom that is essential. There's no category in Scripture for membership in a parachurch; so help your people, especially your young people, to love the local church.

Secondly, do not merely outsource ministry. Disciple your church. Teach your people. Use your church as a platform for evangelism. Do not be afraid of reinventing the wheel because your church is God's Plan A.

Lastly, support healthy parachurch ministries. The local church can benefit from the specialization of the parachurch, and the parachurch needs the generalization of the local church. Lead your people to parachurch ministries that love the church and come alongside the church to accomplish the Great Commission.

Sam Crites serves as the lead pastor of Mosaic Church. He is currently working on his PhD in Historical and Theological Studies at the Southern Baptist Theological Seminary. He and his wife Molly live in College Station, Texas with their five children: Nora Kate, Jacob, Ford, June, and Piper.

Why An Elder Should Oversee the Church Bookstall

Josh Manley

As a lover of history, walking through a museum with rare artifacts thrills me. Museums collect the best artifacts by depending on experts who know their field and seek to tell a trustworthy story.

What does a museum have to do with your church bookstall or library? I am glad you asked.

Both should collect instructive and enjoyable resources. Neither should curate content that fails to give a deeper grasp of reality. When your church's bookstall overseer isn't feeding the sheep healthy food, they're working against the digestion of the church's entire teaching ministry.

Pastors, the world of Christian and pseudo-Christian books is overwhelming. Please don't let your people fend for themselves. An elder should oversee your church bookstall. Why?

1. THE BOOKSTALL MAGNIFIES YOUR TEACHING MINISTRY.

I was always amazed by the errant publications that made their way into the "Christian" section of brick-and-mortar bookstores. While the employees who stocked the shelves may have had good intentions, they did not necessarily have a pastoral ability or responsibility to teach the Word. But you do, pastor. The books your church sells or gives away are an extension of your teaching ministry.

Just like when your people walk through a Smithsonian museum, they should be able to trust that your bookstall will teach the truth. We often think teaching "what accords with sound doctrine" and protects the flock from "fierce wolves" happens exclusively in the pulpit (Titus 2:1; Acts 20:29). But even though the pulpit is the primary way you teach God's people, it's not your only tool. The books your church offers will either complement or undermine all your tireless effort in the pulpit.

As pastors, we should love our people by filling the bookstall with reliable books and explaining to the church why we included these books and not others. In doing so, you connect in your people's minds the doctrine your church teaches gathered with the books they should read scattered. Each book is a wonderful chance to extend your church's teaching ministry.

2. THE BOOKSTALL DEVELOPS DISCERNMENT.

Bank tellers learn to spot counterfeit bills by closely examining the genuine article. Similarly, a side effect of steeping in reliable resources is developing an allergy to bogus ones. Good books don't just convey content—they train our sensibilities to discern between the good and the bad. They even help our members identify the areas in which they should grow in knowledge and obedience.

Use the ministry of books to feed your sheep and refine their Christian palates. There are many arenas in which Christians should deepen their faith. A well-curated bookstall helps guard and guide your people in matters of orthodoxy—from subjects like biblical theology to disciplining children, from church history to counseling. Use your bookstall to introduce your people to good authors and foundational genres. After all, they may not encounter such books on their own.

3. THE BOOKSTALL FACILITATES DISCIPLESHIP.

Through a well-curated book offering you can provide resources that will equip fathers and mothers to disciple their families, friends to disciple one another, and small group leaders to guide their groups in truth. Elders only have so many man hours. Good books can serve like bumpers in bowling, helping to keep church members within the lines and encouraging them to engage each other with the Word and its application.

Discernment is the friend of discipleship. As your flock reads well, it will make them better thinkers and teachers. And that will strengthen the witness of your church.

4. THE BOOKSTALL ADDRESSES PASTORAL ISSUES.

Websites may offer great resources, but they don't know your flock's particular needs. Maybe you know your church is weak in its understanding of sound doctrine or ecclesiology. Maybe many in your congregation are struggling with pornography or greed.

Good books help pastors care for those for whom they will give an account (Heb. 13:17). They help you shepherd the flock that is among *you* (1 Pet. 5:2). Someone in your church may be hesitant to talk with you about their struggles or sins but willing to pick up a book you have recommended.

As Christians, we are first and foremost people of the Book. But we should also be a people who use good books that explain and apply the Book. So, fellow pastors, don't neglect overseeing the resources your church is, or could be, offering. From the Gutenberg printing press that supported the Reformation to the online articles and books that are at our fingertips today, don't underestimate how our Lord can use written words for the good of his people and the glory of his name. As those entrusted with the oversight of eternal souls, the elders don't just have the *responsibility* to oversee what the church reads—they have the *privilege*.

Josh Manley is a Pastor of RAK Evangelical Church in the United Arab Emirates. You can find him on Twitter at @JoshPManley.

Spotting, Assessing, and Training Leaders for Church Ministries

Joel Kurz

"Help! I don't see any leaders!"

I know the feeling. Pastors often struggle finding leaders for church ministries. We need them, but we don't see them. And even if we saw, we'd be unable to train them fast enough to meet the rising demands of ministry.

After a few years pastoring, it's easy to become jaded about this. Like a sleight-of-hand magician playing with our mind—"Now you see them, now you don't"—we ask, "Where did all the leaders go? What happened to all of yesterday's exciting prospects?" We thought they'd stick around and help with the work. As we number the names of potential ministry leaders who fizzled out over the years, we are tempted to feel discouraged.

A lack of leaders strains the staff—especially the pastors— and discourages ministry leaders who need help. It limits our ability to reach the lost, care for the hurting, and make disciples.

We need to find and train leaders. But how?

YOU'RE NOT ALONE, BUT YOU MUST PRAY

Let's start with the bad news: the laborers are few. This has been a problem for at least two thousand years. In Matthew 9, Jesus' heart broke for the crowds who were like sheep without a shepherd, "Then he said to his disciples, 'The harvest is plentiful, but the laborers are few'" (Matt. 9:37). Let this serve as an encouragement: you're not alone.

As we (sinfully) compare our ministries to others, we assume they have more leaders, better workers, and unending help. I propose that this is simply untrue. We all struggle to spot and train new workers. "Few laborers" is everyone's reality. We're in this together.

So what do we do? We pray. It's important to note what Jesus *didn't* say. He did not say, "The laborers are few, so go recruit from other churches, start an internship, or launch an annual training program." No, Jesus' primary program for leadership development is prayer. The laborers are few; "therefore pray earnestly to the Lord of the harvest to send out laborers into his harvest" (Matt. 9:38).

Pastor, are you praying for ministry leaders? As your heart breaks with compassion for the sheep and burns with desire for the harvest, do you fall before the God of the harvest in prayer and beg him for laborers? Do you pray for eyes to see who you may train, even now, in your own congregation?

YOU HAVE WHAT YOU NEED, BUT YOU MUST TRAIN

They're already among us. As we pray for laborers, let us recognize that God has already gifted the church with what she needs. The future laborers we are praying for may be in our midst. We are one body, with many members. "We have different gifts, according to the grace given to each of us" (Rom. 12:6).

In Ephesians 4, God gives officers to the church for the purpose of equipping "the saints for the work of ministry." In Titus 2, Pastor Titus is instructed to train up the older men and women in the faith so "they can urge the younger" (Titus 2:4).

The New Testament example encourages us to look within, be thankful for who we already have, and train them to do the work of ministry. The superhero ministry leader of your dreams may not be coming. Yet you have a whole congregation of ordinary aunts, uncles, grandpas, students, retirees, and blue-collar workers among you—regular folks whom God has remade as building blocks for his temple.

TWO PRINCIPLES

1. Start with people, not programs.

If I may humbly offer a few don'ts: don't start with an internship. Don't start with a leadership pipeline program. Don't start by outsider recruitment. If you're not already doing the work of training the saints, just start there.

I also mean this as a word of encouragement. You don't need a silver-bullet program. You have been gifted with regenerate members whom God has gifted particularly for your church. There is a time and place to recruit workers from other churches (Lord willing, in partnership with those churches). You may be wise to eventually start an internship or build a pipeline. But first, trust that God has already equipped his church with future ministry leaders.

2. Train those who will respond to your training, and who will then train others.

Before he hosted a formal internship program, Mark Dever explained his discovery process of new trainees in this way:

Taking my sermon preparation very seriously; praying for evangelism and discipling; trying to model that by befriending non-Christians; sharing the gospel with them; befriending members of the church and trying to help them grow in Christ; watching who responds to my work, who picks up on the pattern, and who begins to reduplicate what I do with others; praying in particular for those brothers.[13]

Personally, I pour into everyone I can, and then I see who responds. We demystify leadership development in this way. Begin with training through modeling, explain what you do and why you do it, and then pour additional time and resources into those who:

1. Respond to your work.
2. Pick up on the pattern.
3. Begin to reduplicate what you do with others.

---

13 Dever, "How to Raise Up Pastors" https://www.9marks.org/article/how-do-pastors-raise-pastors/

WHAT DO WE DO?

How should I train my ministry leaders? Let's go back to Paul's instructions to Pastor Titus:

1. Train them by your example (Titus 2:7).

I don't know of a better "program" than spending time with the trainee. When participating in a particular task, bring them along with you. Show them how you fold the bulletins and pass it on. When you work on the annual budget, don't do it alone. When attending a lunch meeting or counseling session, if appropriate, bring a trainee. Let them see you at your best and your worst. When they see you at your worst, model repentance and humility.

2. Train them to be temperate (Titus 2:2).

This means self-restraint and a clear mind. Ministry is often filled with drama and unpopular decisions. A sober-mind is important. Extremism is a threat. Consider using ministry-dilemma case studies with the trainee. Walk them through principles of biblical wisdom.

3. Train them to be worthy of respect (Titus 2:8).

Personal holiness is of utmost importance. When a ministry leader fails, it's not always due to lack of skill. They fizzle due to sinful distractions, temptations, the inability to be refreshed in the Word, or moral failure. In addition, some leaders would be more effective if they simply grew in self-awareness, approachability, compassion, warmth, and people skills. Many otherwise godly men suffer simply because they come across as standoffish, harsh, or uncaring. It's wise to correct ways in which the trainee unintentionally loses the respect of others.

4. Train them to be self-controlled (Titus 2:6).

Paul rewords this admonition for the older women: "not slanderers or addicted to wine." The person who is competent in their job yet fails in their self-control will destroy their ministry. How many churches have suffered because a ministry leader has had a sharp temper and loose tongue? Self-control is not something that can be taught in a class or assessed in an exam. It's caught, taught, and corrected through life together.

5. Train them to be sound in faith, love, and endurance (Titus 2:2).

Paul again rewords this for the women: "train them to teach what is good." How? First, in your own teaching, show integrity and seriousness (2:7). Personally, my goal is to teach the trainee how to read the Bible. Only if they read the Bible correctly can they teach the Bible correctly.

You should also read and discuss good books on doctrine and biblical theology. Read the Bible together and teach inductive Bible study along the way. Discuss sermons with the trainee and receive their feedback. Just as I write this, I have paused to ask Alton, one of our church members, for his feedback on my sermon text for this Sunday. Seek to incorporate training into your regular ministry patterns and day-to-day conversations.

Yes, the laborers are few. You're not alone. But the good news is that you already have what it takes to begin training. It's not rocket science. You don't need a new program or an expensive residency. Simply pass on to others what has been given to you (2 Tim. 2:2). rust that God will raise up workers for his church and send laborers into the harvest. And what a harvest we have before us!

Joel Kurz is the lead pastor of The Garden Church in Baltimore, Maryland. You can find him on Twitter at @joelkurz.

How to Encourage Women's Discipling in the Local Church

Madison Hetzler

"Who in your life has been most influential to you and how?"

My family was gathered around a pan of brownies baked over a camp stove when someone posed this question. I listened as my family members mentioned pastors, co-workers, college roommates, and dear friends, celebrating their godly attributes in detail. And yet I found myself convicted. Outside of a few close friends, my life was populated by casual relationships and Bible study groups that lacked real accountability. I thought about how I have stumbled over passages like Titus 2:3–5. The kind of mentorship Paul describes there has seemed elusive. Here I was, a woman who knew and loved the Lord, yet I longed for godly influence and accountability. I was, in a word, lonely.

I'd venture a guess that most Christians have, at some point, felt similarly. Loneliness is a trying thing. Because we are made to dwell in rich community, the lack of it chaps. Women are particularly prone to interpret loneliness as a personal indictment, making its pang even more acute.

Discipling is a beautiful word, and it's the antidote to loneliness in the church. Every Christian wants to be discipled and to disciple others. After all, in Christ, every woman has something to give and something to receive. Discipling is a balm for lonesome living and a gracious rebuke against independence and autonomy. It comforts the worried and counters the self-centered. It challenges the notion that one's church is a place for spectatorship and entertainment. It reinforces the single woman eager for marriage and the mom with little ones about her feet. It also calls women with testimonies of God's faithfulness to pour her stores into others.

Discipling is a gift from our Lord.

WHAT IS DISCIPLING?

Simply put, discipling is helping others follow Jesus. It works to bring others along to maturity in Christ. The mature woman grows in love for and knowledge of the Lord (Phil. 1:9). She bears fruit in keeping with the Spirit (Gal. 5:22-23). And she walks in humble obedience to his commands (2 Jn. 1:6). This kind of maturity may sound like a lofty goal. Still, Christ's work within us enables our progress. How exciting to become more like Christ and help others do the same!

But sadly, in a fallen world, even beautiful, exciting, and wonderful things can often seem inconvenient or unnecessary. We need to recognize discipling as beautiful, yes, but also as essential. The Lord doesn't suggest we disciple, he commands us to do so. It's not ornamental, but vital.

Consider the instruction we receive in Scripture. Colossians 3:16 directs us to admonish one another in wisdom and the teachings of Christ. First Thessalonians 5:14 instructs us to come alongside the mischievous, the tired, and the weak and patiently help her to walk in Christlikeness. Hebrews 3:13 tells us to exhort and protect one another from sin. Again and again, Scripture commands us to help one another. Every Christian woman without exception is made for discipling.

WHERE DO WE FIND DISCIPLING?

What would you think if you were tasked to feed a table full of people using a complicated recipe, but you had no kitchen in which to prepare it? No stove, no knife, no pots and pans. Some of us would feel panic, others hopelessness, and still others would laugh at the predicament and give up altogether. Our definition of discipling is valuable, but we need more than a definition. Thank the Lord that we are not cooks without kitchens but sisters in Christ with the local church.

The local church provides the context to begin obeying the commands God has given us. In the local church, Christians gather to hear the gospel preached. We proclaim the Word and make it visible through baptism and the Lord's Supper. We covenant together and commit to helping one another follow Scripture's commands. We hold one another accountable through exhortation and church discipline. And we are equipped to return to our homes, careers, and friendships and walk in obedience to the Lord. A church clarifies our purpose and provides us with a support structure for giving and receiving help. It offers the fertile ground discipleship needs to flourish. When we sit under the Word together, our discipling relationships gain rich content for discussion, exhortation, and encouragement.

During Sunday services, therefore, you should be attentive to the needs around you. Build relationships with other women and learn where they are in their walk with the Lord. Seek out those behind you and those ahead of you. Remember, you have riches in Christ to give and to receive—and there's no better place than a church to do just that.

Then, let what happens on Sunday spill over into the rest of the week. Share a church pew, then start sharing dinner tables, sidewalks, and car rides. If you are pressed for time, fold others into your schedule. Wonderful discipling happens when you show others what Christlikeness looks like in the ordinary and the hectic. Conversations of eternal value can happen even while folding laundry, going on a run, driving to pick up kids from school, and, of course, sharing the proverbial cup of coffee.

FINALLY, SISTERS

If you are convicted about the lack of intimate discipling in your life, take heart. You don't have to stay in that place, and God doesn't want you to. He doesn't dangle a good gift like discipling and dole out loneliness instead. Scripture's gifts and instruction are by no means inaccessible or an ideal too far off. Rather, in Christ, we are blessed with "every spiritual blessing in the heavenly places" (Eph. 1:3). Pray passages like Titus 2:3–5 and John 13:34–35 back to the Lord and ask him to provide discipling relationships. If you are looking for someone to disciple, remember that other women are praying for someone like you.

Years later, I'm thankful that God did not leave me, brownie in hand, hungry for discipling. If I could go back to that family circle, I would tell them about Linda, a mom of eleven who loves to study the Puritans. Her conscience is soft to the Holy Spirit's prodding, and she draws from a deep well of Scripture memorization in every conversation. She agreed to walk with me weekly at some points and daily at others. She has invested heavily in my walk with Christ, my marriage, and my newfound role as a mother.

I would also tell them about Theresa, a missionary of 40 years who has invited me into her home again and again and has faithfully prayed for and with me for two years. She's bounced my fussing son on her knee and helped me think through topics of great weight, such as a young child's profession of faith.

I would talk about Megan, a young seminary student who is newly engaged. When I share my memories and experiences of that time with her, I find myself remembering lessons the Lord taught me then that I need just as much now.

Praise the Lord for these portraits of God's grace in my life, as well as for the gift of discipling and being discipled.

Madison Hetzler is wife to Josh Hetzler and mother to Graham Hetzler. She is a member of The Heights Baptist Church in South Chesterfield, Virgina, where she serves in a number of capacities. Additionally, Madison loves to write, cook, and play tennis.

Why Pastors Should Oversee the Women's Ministry

Camryn Zamora

O ne of Aesop's fables tells the story of a group of bulls who lived in a field. A lion tried to attack them, but together they drove him off.

One day, the bulls quarreled over a single patch of grass and stubbornly parted ways, getting as far away from each other as possible. The lion seized this opportunity and devoured the bulls one by one.

Women's ministry can sometimes feel like those bulls, each separating into its own "patch of grass" away from the rest of the church. Critics of complementarianism argue that male leadership oppresses women. Perhaps it's tempting for complementarian churches to react to this criticism with a hands-off approach, allowing women's ministries to become a space where women are given independence from the elders—a place for them to exercise their gifts free from the oversight of male pastors.

I am convinced that while this grass may look greener, women, like men, need pastoral oversight and care.

I am a member of the Evangelical Community Church of Abu Dhabi (ECC), where I serve as a deacon of women's ministry. Through the perseverance of faithful saints, ECC has changed and matured over the past fifty years.

When my family first arrived, our church had just undergone a major shift in polity, moving from the leadership of a co-ed administrative "church board" to a plurality of male elders. The women's ministry quickly improved as it came under the care of biblically qualified shepherds.

Previously, the women's ministry operated independently, with its own constitution, membership, and leadership council. It organized its own finances, curriculum, and programs without pastoral input. Women leaders did their best to minister to women, and by God's grace, their efforts bore fruit. Women formed bonds of loving fellowship, and some grew in their knowledge of God.

But the women suffered from a lack of pastoral oversight. It was common for women, even church members, to attend women's events but never corporate worship. Many ladies saw women's ministry as their church rather than a ministry within the church. Some of the lessons and curriculum were unsound. Disputes arose between leaders. On one occasion, a woman gave a talk that she had plagiarized from a notorious false teacher.

But perhaps the greatest harm was to women who were trapped in crippling sin or broken situations. They did not receive pastoral attention because their cases remained isolated.

When I became a member of ECC, things were just beginning to change as the newly appointed elders began overseeing ministries within the church. Since our women's ministry has come under pastoral care, the women in our church have been equipped, nurtured, united, and protected far better than they were when they functioned autonomously.

Why? Here's a brief look at the reason behind each of these benefits.

BIBLICALLY EQUIPPED

Our churches need theologically sound women. Sisters who are equipped and eager to disciple other women are a tremendous benefit to the entire body. Therefore, the church should strive to create a culture of women who can rightly handle the Word and disciple others to do the same. Pastoral oversight is the most assured path not only to equipping the female saints but also to building a culture of discipleship in which sisters feel competent and commissioned to minister to each other.

At ECC, elders equip women in various ways. The absolute best way a pastor loves the women in the church is to ensure they are being taught the Word through faithful preaching and teaching. Our pastors also welcome us to classes alongside pastoral interns, encourage our participation in Simeon Trust workshops, and even provide feedback on manuscripts before we publicly teach one another. These supports communicate our elders' deep commitment to the women in the congregation. They want our ladies to flourish under the rich biblical teaching of well-taught sisters so that we can foster a discipleship culture (Titus 2:3).

As a beneficiary of faithful shepherding, I rejoice in Ephesians 4:11–12, that Christ gave us shepherds "to equip the saints for the work of ministry, for building up the body of Christ." Our elders haven't bought our contentment by staying out of our way, and they value our members too much to "live and let live." Instead, they invest time and resources into us so that we are well-equipped to disciple other women.

When pastors ensure sound doctrine in women's ministry, it does not demean women as inferior. Rather, they are lovingly treating us as fellow image-bearers of God and co-heirs of Christ.

LOVINGLY NURTURED

While corporate worship is where our souls are best cared for, we also need to be individually nurtured. When pastors oversee women's ministry, they ensure that no woman suffers in silence. Women may have a strong support system through their sisters, but how much sweeter is it to be loved and cared for by not only sisters but also brothers?

Pastoral oversight ensures that sisters are being cared for by the whole body. The body grows up into Christ when it is held together by *every* joint with which it is equipped (Eph. 4:15–16). Paul intervened in Philippi to urge Euodia and Syntyche to agree in the Lord. These women partnered with Paul, and he cares for them enough to entreat the church to get involved in their reconciliation.

Because our pastors at ECC oversee the women's ministry, they know the needs of our sisters. It is commonplace for them to take the initiative to ask a mature woman to meet with a sister who is struggling. And likewise, we communicate the needs of our sisters to our elders, so that they can pray and minister to us.

Women aren't silos, only ministering to and being ministered to by women. We are a part of a family of brothers and sisters, who care for each other's needs under the biblically prescribed leadership of our pastors.

HARMONIOUSLY UNIFIED

It is true that elders cannot minister to women in the same way women can. However, women need pastoral oversight to minister to each other well. We need their guidance on matters of budget, calendar, curriculum choices, etc.

We need oversight in these areas because the church functions as one body. Our pastors know the church from a special vantage point: they see the entire body. They have to oversee what is best not just for the hands, but also for the feet. They must consider whether an event will strengthen the entire body, or if it will serve only a few; and when to focus on the needy rather than the well (1 Cor. 12:21–26). They pay attention to when the body is bleeding in places the rest of us cannot see. So, we do well to trust their leadership and submit to them as they oversee even some of the more mundane matters of the ministry.

At ECC, we choose our curriculum with our pastors. There have been times we've wanted to study one topic, but the pastors asked us to study another topic that they felt would be a greater benefit to our sisters in that season. We have never regretted going with their recommendation.

Our elders have James 3:1 as a sobering reminder: teachers will face stricter judgement. Pastors shoulder that burden for us by ensuring that what we study is biblically sound. There is mutual respect and collaboration, and their oversight lifts a burden that autonomy unnecessarily places on ministries.

FAITHFULLY PROTECTED

Perhaps the greatest benefit to pastoral oversight is that it safeguards the women in the church. Hebrews 13:17 says, "Obey your leaders and submit to them, for they are *keeping watch over your souls*, as those who will have to give an account."

The idea of "keeping watch" reminds me of what my husband does every time we walk together. He puts me on the inside of the path, placing himself between the nearest danger and me. This isn't done with ill intent. He's not communicating that he's stronger or more capable; he's placing my life before his own.

Good pastors routinely do the same for us, which is why it's a delight to submit to them. They stand between the flock and the influence of false teachers. Paul charged the Ephesian elders to guard the precious flock of Christ from wolves (Acts 20:28–30).

When our pastors oversee women's ministry, it doesn't indicate distrust, but rather that *when the wolves attack, the shepherds will bear the brunt, not the sheep.* In doing so, they imitate the Good Shepherd, who lays down his life for his sheep (John 10:11–15).

THE DIVINE DESIGN

All of this displays God's good and glorious design for his church. In his sovereign wisdom, the gospel is beautifully displayed when we humbly submit to pastoral leadership and rejoice in God's kindness for giving us these men. Keri Folmar writes, "Your happy submission to elder authority will be to your own advantage. You will thrive, and your elders will serve you and the church body with joy."[14]

So, while it might be tempting to view pastoral oversight as restrictive for women since we don't occupy the office of elder, my experience has been radically different. Robust pastoral oversight has communicated love, care, and value to our female members. And when women seek an "autonomous space" to exercise their independence and leadership, they are in fact splitting from the herd, placing themselves in danger of being picked off.

Pastors, some women may be tempted to find their own patch of grass, but please, for the sake of the gospel and our souls, don't let us!

Camryn Zamora is a deacon of women's ministry at Evangelical Community Church in Abu Dhabi.

---

14 Keri Folmer, *How Can Woman Thrive in the Local Church?* (Crossway, 2021).

Build on Jesus

BY DEEPAK REJU & MARTY MACHOWSKI

Deepak Reju & Marty Machowski, *Build on Jesus: A Comprehensive Guide to Gospel-Based Children's Ministry*. New Growth Press, 2021. 208 pages.

Connie Dever

I f my husband Mark Dever were to add a "mark" of a healthy church regarding children's ministry, the book *Build on Jesus* could be the practical guide to living it out. This is the children's ministry book I've been waiting for. I have given out hundreds of copies since it was released last year.

To whom have I given them? Some have gone to children's ministry workers and administrators, as you would expect. But primarily, I try to get this book in the hands of pastors.

Here's why: *Build on Jesus* does more than provide good advice on topics you'd expect to find in a children's ministry book. It also explains the need for pastoral oversight of children's ministry and how to provide it.

TERRIFIC ON TYPICAL TOPICS

Getting teachers to teach, getting kids to learn—this is where children's ministry books usually spill ink. These are important topics and *Build On Jesus* has wonderful sections devoted to them.

Chapter 1 lays an important foundation, defining what God calls us to teach the children: his Word and his gospel. The book gives advice on choosing, creating, and using curriculum in ways that are not only faithful to Scripture, but also enjoyable and memorable to kids.

Chapters 8-10 discuss how to maintain a safe teaching environment. The crucial first step can take place before teaching. These chapters glean highlights about protecting our children and those who work with them from Deepak's bigger book *On Guard*. Chapter 11 is rich with practical advice on managing the classroom that can help any teacher. In Chapter 12, Marty writes on the importance of creativity in the teaching environment, which was thought-provoking and unique.

Build On Jesus is a worthwhile read simply for what these men have to say regarding these typical children's ministry book topics. The concise chapters and evaluation questions might even get your busy, volunteer teachers to read it.

A CALL TO PASTORS

But the reason I've given out so many copies of *Build on Jesus* to pastors isn't for the topics mentioned above. It's because this book does something few (if any) other children's ministry books do; it provides pastors with the healthy, biblical, church-centered framework they need to lead children's ministry well.

Why should pastors spend their time on children's ministry? Here are five reasons:

1. Pastors will be held accountable for the soundness of the teaching that takes place under their leadership, and surely this includes what is taught in children's ministry.
2. Children's ministry frequently enlists more members than any other ministry in the church. And often, their volunteering takes place during worship services or adult classes. Someone needs to make sure the volunteers are nourishing their own souls.
3. Most members become parents, meaning children's ministry is a great way to support a large portion of the congregation.
4. Ages 4–14 are a fertile time of conversion and, unfortunately, of false conversion. Pastors help discern the difference and keep the gospel clear.

5. Everyone in a church is a child or was a child.

A pastor's ministry *is* children's ministry. One way or another, everyone in their church is affected. Pastors are called by God to know, feed, and equip the sheep. Who better than they to oversee this ministry that has such widespread impact!

Yet often, pastors are overwhelmed or unsure how to do so. *Build on Jesus* does an excellent job of helping pastors understand how to provide this leadership.

A PASTOR'S JOB DESCRIPTION: FAMILY-EQUIPPING

You have probably heard of the family-integrated approach to children's ministry, which places the responsibility of teaching children largely— if not solely—within the nuclear family. Part of the popularity of that approach is in response to parents wrongly "outsourcing" their God-given responsibility to others. Amen to that!

Build on Jesus is also a response to parents shirking their God-given responsibilities, but it presents a "family-equipping" model. In this approach, parents are equipped and supported as the spiritual nurturers of their children, *by* the members of their local church, under the leadership and guidance of the pastors.

But their model isn't only a "family-equipping" model; it is a "nourish-every-soul" model, too, providing advice on how to care for families and provide childcare and children's Bible classes without burning out teachers, and especially your children's ministry director (CMD). Did you know that the average CMD lasts in their position only three years before burning out? Reading chapter five and implementing its wisdom can help you care well for your CMD, for the sake of his or her own soul, as well as the sake of your children's ministry.

If you are a church planting pastor, you have the hardest job of all. There is pressure on you to "build the children's ministry plane in the air," and you're tempted to toss children's ministry to your wife. This book is filled with the wisdom you need to build your children's ministry before it takes flight, even when there is pressure on you to hurry up and have kids' programs. Appendix A is a special section written with you in mind.

I'm telling you, pastors, this book is written for *you* as much as your children's ministry workers, if not more so. Buy this book for chapters 4 and 5 and Appendix A alone! And do not simply hand it off to your CMD. Buy two copies and discuss it with them. If there's no time to read the whole book, focus on Chapters 4 and 5 and Appendix A.

A WHOLE CHURCH AFFAIR

Let me close with a favorite quote from the book:

> That's how the church should work—it's not just parents, but every adult who walks in the doors of the church building, every adult who talks to a kid after church, every volunteer in childcare, every Sunday school teacher, every hall monitor—each and every one has an opportunity to communicate the glories of our great God to these children. You don't have to be in a more formal role, like a preacher or a Sunday School teacher, to be a conveyor of truth to church kids. The hope and prayer is that one generation will tell of the Lord to the next generation, and that generation will tell the next. (28)

Pastors, church members, parents: your ministry *is* children's ministry. *Build on Jesus* is a book that can help you build tomorrow's healthy church today.

I should know. I have spent my life working in children's ministry under Deepak and the other elders at Capitol Hill Baptist Church with the model presented in this book. I have had the blessing of being personally shepherded well by it and watching our church thrive under it.

Connie Dever is the wife of Mark Dever, pastor of Capitol Hill Baptist Church in Washington, DC.

* 9 7 8 1 9 5 8 1 6 8 7 3 8 *